OCCASIONAL PAPER 146

Thailand
The Road to Sustained Growth

Kalpana Kochhar, Louis Dicks-Mireaux, Balazs Horvath,
Mauro Mecagni, Erik Offerdal, and Jianping Zhou

D0879370

INTERNATIONAL MONETARY FUND
Washington DC
December 1996

© 1996 International Monetary Fund

Library of Congress Cataloging-in-Publication Data

Thailand : the road to sustained growth / Kalpana Kochhar . . . [et al.].
      p.   cm. — (Occasional paper ; no. 146)
   Includes bibliographic references (p.   ).
   ISBN 1-55775-603-1
    1. Structural adjustment (Economic policy)—Thailand. 2. Thailand—
Economic policy. 3. Thailand—Economic conditions I. Kochhar,
Kalpana. II. Series: Occasional paper (International Monetary Fund) ;
no. 146.
HC445.T44997   1996
338.9593—dc20   96-48790
                                                CIP

Price: US$15.00
(US$12.00 to full-time faculty members and
students at universities and colleges)

Please send orders to:
International Monetary Fund, Publication Services
700 19th Street, N.W., Washington, D.C. 20431, U.S.A.
Tel.: (202) 623-7430   Telefax: (202) 623-7201
Internet: publications@imf.org

recycled paper

Contents

The following symbols have been used throughout this paper:

. . . to indicate that data are not available;

— to indicate that the figure is zero or less than half the final digit shown, or that the item does not exist;

– between years or months (for example, 1991–92 or January–June) to indicate the years or months covered, including the beginning and ending years or months;

/ between years (for example, 1991/92) to indicate a crop or fiscal (financial) year.

"Billion" means a thousand million.

Minor discrepancies between constituent figures and totals are due to rounding.

The term "country," as used in this paper, does not in all cases refer to a territorial entity that is a state as understood by international law and practice; the term also covers some territorial entities that are not states, but for which statistical data are maintained and provided internationally on a separate and independent basis.

Preface

Only thirty years ago, Thailand was among the world's poorest economies. In the period since the mid-1960s, the Thai economy has witnessed remarkably strong and resilient growth despite several adverse shocks. This paper, prepared by staff in the Policy Development and Review Department, is one of the country studies completed as input to *Reinvigorating Growth in Developing Countries: Lessons from Adjustment Policies in Eight Economies,* Occasional Paper 139, which examines the response of growth and investment to adjustment policies since the early 1970s. The latter study was also prepared by a staff team in the Policy Development and Review Department, led by David Goldsbrough.

The authors of the present study would like to acknowledge the valuable input and guidance of David Goldsbrough and the helpful suggestions from Susan Schadler, Ken Bercuson, Sharmini Coorey, and Elie Canetti. Kadima Kalonji provided outstanding research assistance, and Olivia Carolin and Fernanda Gusmão provided excellent secretarial assistance. The authors are also grateful to James McEuen of the External Relations Department, who edited the paper and coordinated its publication.

The views expressed here, as well as any errors, are the sole responsibility of the authors and do not necessarily reflect the opinion of the government of Thailand, the Executive Directors of the IMF, or other members of the IMF staff.

The study was completed in June 1995 and, for the most part, is based on information available up to that time.

1 Overview

Thailand's growth performance during the past three decades has been remarkable by any yardstick. Like most low-income developing countries, Thailand was severely affected by the external shocks of the late 1970s and early 1980s. Unlike many developing countries in which these shocks proved to be highly destabilizing, however, Thailand showed remarkable resilience. Price stability was quickly restored, and the Thai economy emerged from this period with a strong recovery in growth and investment in an environment of overall macroeconomic stability (Figure 1). This paper examines Thailand's macroeconomic and structural policies and the evolution of growth and investment, with a view to understanding the main factors that led to this successful outcome.

The next section discusses the main factors underlying Thailand's long-term growth performance, factor accumulation, and productivity trends, in the context of cross-country econometric studies. The paper then focuses on the behavior of key macroeconomic variables in response to the shocks of the late 1970s and early 1980s, during the ensuing adjustment period in the first half of the 1980s, and during the surge in capital inflows in the second half of the 1980s. It also previews the major macroeconomic and structural policy responses to these shocks. Next, the paper undertakes a detailed examination of the role of policies—fiscal, monetary, exchange rate, and structural—in the adjustment

Figure 1. Selected Economic Indicators

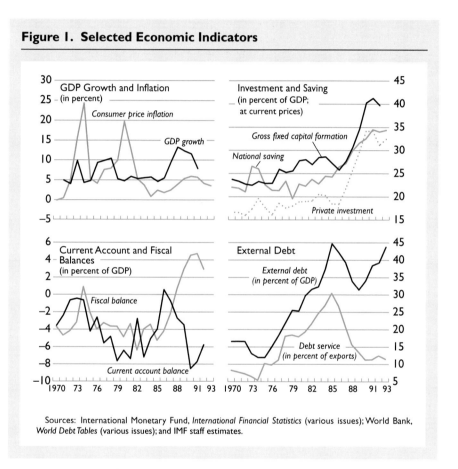

Sources: International Monetary Fund, *International Financial Statistics* (various issues); World Bank, *World Debt Tables* (various issues); and IMF staff estimates.

process.[1] A detailed econometric study of private investment behavior in Thailand is provided in the appendix.

[1]Throughout this paper, the adjustment period in Thailand is treated as the period between 1981 and 1986, which also coincides with the period during which Thailand's adjustment efforts were supported by the IMF and the World Bank. Thailand had three IMF stand-by arrangements—in June 1981, November 1982, and June 1985—together with drawings under the IMF's compensatory and contingency financing facility (CCFF) and buffer stock financing facility, and two structural adjustment loans from the World Bank (in May 1982 and March 1983). Owing to a marked improvement in Thailand's economic circumstances, particularly the balance of payments position, the Thai authorities decided to cancel the last IMF stand-by arrangement as of January 1, 1987.

II   Long-Term Growth Performance

Thailand's economic growth performance during the past three decades has been impressive. In 1960, per capita gross domestic product (GDP) was only slightly higher than that in India, Pakistan, Ghana, and Morocco and lower than that in Sri Lanka, the Philippines, Argentina, Chile, and Peru. By 1992, however, with per capita GDP estimated at nearly US$4,000 (valued at purchasing-power-parity—PPP—prices), Thailand had far surpassed the average for South Asia as well as that of many Latin American countries that began the period with higher per capita incomes, and it had reduced the gap with its high-performing East Asian neighbors.

Thailand has also been successful in *diversifying its economic structure* in a relatively short period of time. Between 1970 and the late 1980s, the agricultural sector's contribution to GDP declined from 25 percent of GDP to 15 percent, while that of the manufacturing sector rose from 25 percent to about 35 percent. Significant diversification took place in the structure of exports, with the share of agricultural products falling more than half (to below 30 percent) in the late 1980s, when manufactured goods, especially textiles and garments, surpassed rice as the highest export earner. The manufacturing sector's share of the labor force remained virtually unchanged, however, reflecting trade and industrial policies that, until the mid-1980s, had favored capital-intensive manufacturing.

Key Features of Economic Policies

The most striking feature of Thailand's economic policy environment is its record of *macroeconomic stability*. For most of the past three decades, Thailand has followed conservative macroeconomic policies in support of its policy of maintaining (de jure or de facto) a fixed exchange rate (with the exception of two nominal devaluations in 1981 and 1984). Except for two brief periods immediately following the two oil price shocks, inflation has been in the single digits, and since 1982 it has averaged less than 4 percent. Although it could be ar-

gued that the adjustment to the external shocks of the 1970s and early 1980s was initially slow (see Section III), the imbalances were not permitted to become so acute as to undermine the credibility of policymakers.

The prevailing view among Thai policymakers has always been that the government should play only a limited role in the economy and that the private sector should be the engine of growth. Therefore, Thailand's *public enterprise sector* is small, more focused on traditional public sector activities, and more profitable than in many developing countries (see Section VII for details). Furthermore, over time, public sector activity has shifted away from direct involvement in industrial production toward the provision of public infrastructure and services. This, together with the consistently pro-business orientation of the government reflected in its tax laws and industrial policy, has served to create a dynamic private sector.

Thailand's *trade and investment* policies have been characterized by a liberal attitude toward foreign investment inflows, and by a trade system that, albeit oriented toward import substitution until the mid-1980s, had overall protection levels that were moderate in comparison with those of many other developing countries (see Section VII). The government pursued an activist policy of intervening to promote particular industries, with incentives granted by the Board of Investment (BOI) as the most powerful tool of industrial policy. Import substitution and promotion of capital-intensive manufacturing dominated the strategy of industrial development during the 1960s and 1970s. Tariff rates were progressively increased during the 1970s as a response to growing balance of payments difficulties, and there was a proliferation of exemptions and surcharges on specific products and some nontariff barriers. Although the strategy of industrialization through import substitution began to be deemphasized in the early 1980s, it was not until the mid-1980s that a decisive break was made away from import substitution and toward export promotion.

Implications of Empirical Studies on the Determinants of Growth

What can we learn about Thailand's growth record from empirical studies of the determinants of long-term growth? In what follows, three questions are addressed. The first seeks to conduct an "accounting for long-run growth" exercise for Thailand, based on cross-country regressions and using data averaged over the period 1960–92. The second uses cross-country estimates of correlations between growth, capital accumulation, and productivity changes, on the one hand, and macroeconomic and structural policies and conditions, on the other, to examine whether Thailand's policy environment has generally been conducive to growth and investment. The third examines the behavior of growth during Thailand's "adjustment" phases after controlling for the long-run determinants of growth identified by the first approach.

More specifically, the first approach is to relate the average annual growth of real per capita GDP to the rates of physical and human capital accumulation, while controlling for population growth and initial real per capita income in each country relative to that of the United States (to capture the prediction that less technologically advanced countries tend to catch up over time with more advanced ones).[2] The results of such an exercise are shown in Table 1. On the basis of this cross-section regression, Thailand's rate of factor accumulation and its relatively low initial income level could have been expected to yield average per capita income growth of about 2.6 percent a year between 1960 and 1992; actual average annual growth over this period was 4.5 percent, suggesting that about 40 percent of long-term growth in Thailand is attributable to influences other than the accumulation of factors of production, including productivity gains not related to those arising from the "catching-up" phenomenon. This outcome is similar to that for most of the rest of East Asia.

Many caveats apply when interpreting the results of such empirical analyses: first, the regression explains less than one-half of the variation in per capita income growth across countries (see Table 1); second, the approach is based on the assumption that all countries have the same production function; third, the quality of the data for several countries is poor, and it is impossible to identify the direction of biases so introduced. Although the results need to be interpreted with care, they do imply that—compared

with world "average" growth, adjusted for factor inputs and initial conditions—Thailand's performance has been good, suggesting that, inter alia, the policy environment has by and large been growth enhancing.

The second approach, following Fischer (1993), seeks to identify the effects of macroeconomic and structural policies on output growth, and the channels—capital accumulation or productivity growth—through which these effects are transmitted. From a growth-accounting perspective, output growth can be attributed to increases in the supply of factors and to a residual total factor productivity (TFP).[3]

Several proxy measures were used for the impact of policies, and correlations were examined between these proxies and output growth, factor accumulation, and TFP growth, respectively, in a cross-country and time-series regression analysis.[4] The panel regressions indicate that macroeconomic instability—measured by the rate of inflation—is negatively associated with growth, and that this link works through both capital accumulation and productivity (Table 2). Overall policy uncertainty or intervention in the exchange system—indicated by the parallel market exchange rate premium—is also negatively correlated with growth, with most of the effect acting through capital accumulation.

The results also suggest that budget surpluses are positively correlated with productivity growth but negatively correlated with capital accumulation. However, examination of the separate influences of government saving and government capital spending reveals that—as would be expected—both components of the overall fiscal balance are positively correlated with capital accumulation. The negative correlation of the budget surplus is accounted for by the

---

[2]This specification is generally associated with theories of endogenous growth, but it is also consistent with the transitional dynamics of a neoclassical growth model that incorporates human capital.

[3]Assuming a constant returns-to-scale production function, TFP growth is calculated by subtracting from output growth the contributions made by the accumulation of capital and growth in the labor force, with the further assumption that the factor shares in the production function are roughly equal to the factor shares in income (that is, 0.4 and 0.6 for capital and labor, respectively). A set of alternative estimates was also prepared using a production function that includes human capital, following the approach of Mankiw, Romer, and Weil (1992). Several other studies have estimated the coefficients of the production function using cross-country data (for example, Knight, Loayza, and Villanueva, 1992; World Bank, 1991; and Elias, 1991). Estimates of TFP using these various approaches are typically highly correlated.

[4]In practice, it is difficult to construct measures of variables that are directly controlled by policies. Researchers therefore proxy policies or distortions by using variables that can be the outcome of policies, but that can also be affected by other (non-policy-related) factors. Thus, the policy implications of the observed linkages between these proxy variables and growth should be drawn with caution. Also, the estimated equations are in no sense "structural equations"; the estimated coefficients can be interpreted only as measures of partial correlations, after controlling for the effects of some other measures of macroeconomic policies and structural conditions.

Table 1. Growth and Factor Accumulation in Thailand and Selected East Asian Countries, 1960–92

	Parameter Estimate	Thailand		Malaysia		Singapore		Hong Kong	
		Sample mean	Contribution	Sample mean	Contribution	Sample mean	Contribution	Sample mean	Contribution
CONSTANT	-0.069		-0.07		0.07		-0.07		-0.07
INV	0.128	18.35	2.35	23.78	3.04	31.81	4.07	19.76	2.53
POPG	-0.190	2.46	-0.47	2.56	0.49	1.68	-0.32	2.01	-0.38
GAP60	-3.771	0.10	-0.36	0.14	0.54	0.17	-0.63	0.23	-0.86
PRIM60	1.228	0.83	1.02	0.96	1.18	1.11	1.36	0.87	1.07
SEC60	0.742	0.12	0.09	0.19	0.14	0.32	0.24	0.24	0.18
Estimated total			2.6		3.3		4.7		2.5
Actual			4.5		4.4		6.4		6.2

	Parameter Estimate	Korea		Taiwan Province of China		Philippines		Indonesia	
		Sample mean	Contribution	Sample mean	Contribution	Sample mean	Contribution	Sample mean	Contribution
CONSTANT	-0.069		-0.07		-0.07		-0.07		-0.07
INV	0.128	24.24	3.10	22.22	2.85	15.44	1.98	17.43	2.23
POPG	-0.190	1.80	-0.34	2.11	-0.40	2.61	-0.50	2.12	-0.40
GAP60	-3.771	0.09	-0.34	0.13	-0.48	0.11	-0.43	0.06	-0.24
PRIM60	1.228	0.94	1.15	0.96	1.18	0.95	1.17	0.67	0.82
SEC60	0.742	0.27	0.20	0.28	0.20	0.26	0.19	0.06	0.04
Estimated total			3.7		3.3		2.3		2.4
Actual			6.7		6.2		1.3		3.7

Source: IMF staff estimates.

Note: The following equation was estimated:

$$GRTH = -0.069 + .128\ INV\ (^{***}) - .190\ POPG + 1.228\ PRIM60\ (^{**}) + .742\ SEC60 - 3.771\ GAP60\ (^{***})$$

(-0.12) (4.40) (-1.18) (2.09) (0.72) (-3.58)

Adjusted R^2 = .45; number of countries: 103.

where GRTH stands for per capita GDP growth, INV refers to the ratio of investment to GDP, POPG is the growth rate of the population (all averaged over the 1960–92 period), GAP60 is the income of country i relative to that of the United States in 1960, and PRIM60 and SEC60 refer to primary and secondary school enrollment rates. Data for GRTH, INV, GAP60, and POPG were taken from the Penn World Table, Mark 5 (Summers and Heston, 1991), and PRIM60 and SEC60 data are from the World Bank's World Tables (various years). *** Implies significance at the 1 percent level, and ** implies significance at the 5 percent level.

Table 2. Impact of Policies on Growth, Capital Accumulation, and Factor Productivity, 1970–92

	Estimated Correlation with Growth[1]	Estimated Correlation with Capital Accumulation[1]	Estimated Correlation with TFP Growth[1]	Thailand	Whole Sample	Asian Developing Countries	East Asia	OECD
Macroeconomic policies								
Inflation	– – –	– – –	– – –	6.7	53.8	9.9	8.1	9.3
Budget surplus[2]	+	– – –	++	–2.6	–4.3	–3.3	–1.6	–4.1
Capital expenditure[2]	+++	+++	...	3.6	4.7	4.8	5.3	2.8
Government saving[2]	+++	+++	++	1.1	0.5	1.4	3.7	–1.2
Exchange rate premium	– – –	– – –	...	—	75.4	48.7	3.8	—
External conditions								
Change in the terms of trade	+++	...	+++	–1.8	—	–0.1	0.9	–0.2
Structural conditions								
Primary school enrollment rate	+++	...	++	81.0	85.1	82.8	95.7	106.0
Ratio of broad money to GDP	...	++	...	47.2	39.0	37.4	47.0	61.4
Average effective trade tax rate[3]	...	– – –	...	7.6	13.4	14.7	12.1	11.6
GDP in 1970 (in logarithms)	– –	– – –	...	3.2	3.3	3.1	3.3	3.9
Memorandum:								
Real GDP growth				6.5	3.4	5.6	7.4	2.7
Growth in real capital stock				8.3	4.2	6.7	9.9	3.6
Growth in total factor productivity (TFP)				1.8	0.3	1.4	1.8	0.7

Source: IMF staff estimates.

[1] The correlations were estimated from three panel regressions with growth in real GDP, capital accumulation, and TFP as dependent variables. TFP residuals were calculated as follows: $TFP = ZGDP - 0.4\ ZKAP - 0.6\ ZLAB$, where $ZGDP$ is the rate of growth of real GDP, $ZKAP$ is the rate of growth in the real capital stock, and $ZLAB$ is the growth rate of the labor force. The data for $ZGDP$ and GDP in 1970 were measured at purchasing-power-parity (PPP) prices and were taken from the Penn World Tables, Mark 5 (Summers and Heston, 1991); data for $ZKAP$ are from King and Levine (1994); data for the budget surplus, government capital expenditure and saving, and the average effective import tax rate are from IMF, *Government Finance Statistics Yearbook* (various years); data for inflation and broad money are from IMF, *International Financial Statistics* (various years); and all other variables are from Fischer (1993). The symbols +++ and – – – mean that the correlations are significant at the 1 percent level; ++(– –) and +(–) imply significance at the 5 and 10 percent levels, respectively.

[2] In percent of GDP. The effects of the budget balances, on the one hand, and capital expenditures and government savings, on the other, were estimated in separate panel regressions. The estimated effects of the other macroeconomic variables did not differ significantly between the two regressions.

[3] Defined as the ratio of total trade taxes to the value of exports and imports.

Table 3. Per Capita Growth Residuals After Controlling for Long-Run Determinants of Growth[1]

(Average growth differential; in percentage points)

	1970–80	1981–86	1987–93
Growth residuals after controlling for investment and other long-run determinants other than "policies"	1.8*** (7.3)	2.7*** (9.1)	6.2*** (15.2)
Growth residuals after controlling for long-run determinants other than investment and "policies"	2.3*** (8.7)	3.4*** (10.8)	8.1*** (21.7)
Growth residuals after controlling for all factors other than investment	2.4 *** (9.2)	3.0*** (9.4)	7.6*** (15.7)

Source: IMF staff estimates.

[1]Following an approach suggested by Bruno and Easterly (1995), the growth residuals were derived by including dummy variables for each country in Barro-style growth regressions (Barro, 1989) estimated using pooled data on the average growth rates over the respective subperiods and across 92 countries. The estimated equations took the following form:

$$GRTH_{it} = \sum_{t=1}^{T} \lambda_t DUM_{it} + \sum_{t=1}^{T} \beta_t DUMI_t + \alpha_1 INV + \alpha_2 POPG + \alpha_3 GAP70 + \alpha_4 PRI70 + \alpha_5 SEC70 .$$

In addition, the following policy-related factors were added to (and *INV* dropped from) the regressors underlying the third set of results reported for each country:

$$\alpha_6 INFL + \alpha_7 BUDSUP + \alpha_8 PREMIUM + \alpha_9 DTOT + \alpha_{10} HINFL,$$

where *T* is the number of subperiods in each case, *GRTH* is the growth rate of real per capita GDP measured in terms of constant domestic prices, *INV* is the share of investment in GDP, *POPG* is the growth rate of the population, *GAP70* is the relative income gap between country *i* and the United States in 1970, *PRI70* and *SEC70* are primary and secondary school enrollment rates in 1970, *INFL* is the average annual rate of inflation in the consumer price index, *BUDSUP* is the government budgetary surplus as a percent of GDP, *PREMIUM* is the average premium between the parallel market and official market exchange rates, and *DTOT* is the change in the ratio of export prices to import prices. Possible nonlinearities in the effects of inflation on growth are taken account of by including the variable *HINFL*, which takes the value of the inflation rate when it is greater than 40 percent. DUM_i are the dummy variables for each period for all countries; and *DUMI* are dummy variables for the country being examined, one for each period. Absolute values of heteroscedastic-consistent *t*-statistics are in parentheses. The symbol *** denotes significance at the 1 percent level, and ** and * at the 5 and 10 percent levels, respectively.

coefficient on capital spending being larger than that on government saving. Moreover, favorable trends in the terms of trade are also strongly associated with output growth. Additional results suggest that high effective trade taxation and an underdeveloped financial system (as measured by the ratio of broad money to GDP) are also negatively correlated with capital accumulation, and that low human capital formation (provided by the primary school enrollment ratio) is negatively correlated with output and productivity growth.

Table 2 presents the estimated correlations of macroeconomic and structural policies with the growth of output capital and TFP growth, and it compares sample averages for the right-hand-side variables for Thailand with those for other countries. By most of the measures, Thailand's macroeconomic policies were—on average during the period, and compared with other regions and countries—

conducive to rapid output growth, capital accumulation, and productivity gains. It would be reasonable to conclude from this evidence that, relative to the behavior of the same variables for other countries, the stable macroeconomic environment—combined with an outward-oriented trade system; a reasonably well-developed and undistorted financial system; and relatively high levels of education, especially at the primary level[5]—have all had a positive influence on Thailand's long-run growth performance. In contrast, the marked deterioration in Thailand's terms of trade could be expected to have had a dampening ef-

---

[5]By contrast, secondary school enrollment rates in Thailand are low and have not increased much over time. As the economy moves toward industries requiring more skilled labor, this may prove to be an impediment to sustained growth. Recognizing this, the authorities have begun to emphasize secondary and higher education in the allocation of public education expenditures.

fect on output growth relative to a situation in which the terms of trade remained stable or improved.[6]

Developments in Output and Productivity During Phases of Adjustment

What happened to output and productivity during the different stages of Thailand's adjustment process, and how do these developments compare with what would be expected on the basis of the long-term determinants of growth set out in Table 1? Following an approach suggested by Bruno and Easterly (1995), this question was addressed by estimating the basic growth regression across a panel of countries during subperiods corresponding to Thailand's adjustment phases (Table 3). The indicated "growth residuals" are a measure of how much Thailand's per capita growth exceeded the world "average" in each subperiod, after controlling for the long-run determinants of growth specified in the equation.

The results indicate that (1) growth was much stronger in Thailand relative to the world average throughout the period under consideration; (2) there was no decline in this growth differential during the period when Thailand was undergoing adjustment—on the contrary, growth remained stronger than the world average; and (3) the growth differential widened markedly during the "postadjustment" period. The equation was reestimated with investment excluded from the set of explanatory variables, to examine whether the change in the growth residual over time reflected influences acting primarily through investment or through productivity. All of these conclusions held true even after omitting investment from the regression. Thus, the impressive economic performance in Thailand, especially in the postadjustment period, could be attributed to productivity gains.

Finally, the equation was reestimated by incorporating a number of macroeconomic policy-related variables—inflation, the budget deficit, and the size of the parallel market premium—as well as changes in the terms of trade. The residuals from this regression give an indication of how much of the differentials in growth between Thailand and the "world" over the adjustment phases can be accounted for by these policy-related variables. The results suggest that, even after taking into account Thailand's macro-

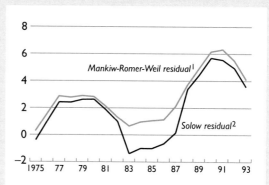

Figure 2. Contribution of Total Factor Productivity to Growth

Sources: International Monetary Fund, *World Economic Outlook* (various issues); World Bank, *World Tables*, "Social Indicators of Development" (various issues); IMF staff estimates; Barro and Lee (1993); Nehru and Dhareshwar (1993); and Sarel (1995).
[1]Residual GDP growth after subtracting the estimated contributions of capital, age-adjusted population growth as an alternative measure of labor force growth, and human capital inputs.
[2]Residual GDP growth after subtracting the estimated contributions of capital and labor, as measured by labor force growth.

economic conditions, growth was significantly higher than the world average, indicating that other policies and conditions contributed to the consistently better-than-average growth performance in Thailand. The size of the growth residuals in each period indicates that the spurt in growth is unlikely to reflect merely a reversion to trend following a temporary slowdown.

Alternative measures of the contributions to growth of TFP, shown in Figure 2, indicate that the acceleration in output growth during the postadjustment phase owed much to a sharp improvement in TFP, in addition to the surge in investment.[7]

---

[6]The factors accounting for the terms of trade deterioration, most of which occurred between 1974 and 1982, are discussed in Section IV.

---

[7]The first measure of TFP growth—the Solow residual—is calculated by assuming a constant returns-to-scale production function and a factor share of 0.4 for capital. The second—the Mankiw-Romer-Weil residual—includes human capital accumulation and an alternative measure of labor force growth—age-adjusted population growth (Sarel, 1995)—and assumes factor shares of 0.33 for each of the three factors of production. Because the labor input measure does not take account of cyclical variations in hours worked, the estimates of TFP incorporate a substantial cyclical component. To correct for this, the contributions of TFP growth shown in the chart are calculated as five-year moving averages. Alternative estimates of Thailand's TFP growth, which make adjustments for improvements in the quality of labor and capital inputs, suggest that TFP growth during this period was somewhat lower than shown here (Tinakorn and Sussangkarn, 1994).

III Economic Developments and Adjustment, 1970–93

The analysis in this section focuses on the shocks of the late 1970s and 1980s. The section also provides an overview of Thailand's economic policy responses to the shocks.

Initial Conditions

During the second half of the 1970s in Thailand, in an attempt to revitalize the economy after the effects of the first oil shock, there was a rapid expansion of public expenditures, and industrial protection and incentives for private investment were increased substantially. Growth and investment picked up, but the public sector deficit widened, in part because prices of energy and other public services were not adjusted in line with costs. The external current account deficit widened dramatically to over 7 percent of GDP in the late 1970s, and external indebtedness rose from below 15 percent of GDP in the mid-1970s to about 35 percent by 1982–83 (Table 4). Thus, the Thai economy was already in a vulnerable position when it was hit with the adverse external shocks of the late 1970s and early 1980s.

Shocks and Responses

During the 1980s the Thai economy faced two sets of macroeconomic shocks. The first set consisted of the second oil price shock in 1979 and the global recession, a decline in commodity prices, and the interest rate hikes of the early 1980s. The second shock was the surge in capital inflows that Thailand has experienced since 1987—in the forms of foreign direct investment from Japan and the Asian newly industrializing economies (NIEs: Hong Kong, Korea, Singapore, and Taiwan Province of China), portfolio capital, and commercial borrowing.

Between 1979 and 1982, the impact of the unfavorable external shocks amounted to a remarkable 11 percentage points of GDP, dominated by the effect of the terms of trade deterioration (equivalent to almost 8 percentage points of GDP).[8] This deterioration arose largely because of the increase in oil prices in 1979–80 and the decline in commodity export prices (primarily of rice) in 1981–82 (Figure 3).

How did the Thai economy respond to these adverse shocks? A useful approach to organizing the discussion of this question has been developed by McCarthy, Neary, and Zanalda (1994). In essence, the methodology involves estimating the impact effects on the balance of payments of the major shocks (changes in the terms of trade, fluctuations in world interest rates, and changes in global demand conditions),[9] and then decomposing the economy's response to these shocks into various measures of adjustment—through changes in export performance and the degree of import intensity or through a demand squeeze affecting the level of economic activity—and changes in the level of external financing.[10] These responses are measured in terms of deviations from historical trends and obviously cannot be attributed simply to changes in policies, since many other factors could have been at work (including the

---

[8]The terms of trade effect is derived as the net impact on the balance of payments from changes in export or import prices (or both), assuming that trade volumes are unchanged.

[9]The estimated impact of global demand shocks is measured by the deviation in world export volume growth from its trend value, and the interest rate effect is measured as the impact of changes in world interest rates on interest payments on the previous year's stock of debt at variable interest rates. The measures of the size of exogenous shocks are based on relatively strong assumptions of other things being equal and should therefore be seen as yielding broad orders of magnitude rather than precise calculations of the impact of shocks.

[10]The estimated change in the real output gap (measured by the difference between actual growth and an estimated trend growth rate) is multiplied by the initial share of imports in GDP in order to calculate a measure of the effect of economic "compression" on the balance of payments. Changes in export performance and import intensity are measured in terms of deviations of actual exports (imports) from simple trade functions, assuming constant income elasticities with respect to partner-country demand (domestic demand). Thus, the exercise involves comparing actual outcomes with a simple counterfactual derived by an extrapolation of past economic relationships (estimated over the preceding five-year period).

Table 4. Key Economic Trends
(Annual average percent change unless otherwise noted)

	1970–73	1974–75	1976–80	1981–86	1987–90	1991–93
Real GDP growth	6.5	4.6	8.0	5.5	11.7	7.8
Real per capita GDP growth	3.4	1.9	5.7	3.4	9.8	6.3
Inflation	6.9	14.8	9.9	4.5	4.4	4.5
Current account balance/GDP	–1.7	–2.4	–5.4	–4.3	–3.8	–6.3
Government balance/GDP	–3.7	–0.2	–3.6	–4.5	1.5	3.2
Investment/GDP[1]	24.6	26.7	27.1	28.5	34.2	40.9
Private	18.2	22.3	19.4	20.1	28.6	33.3
Public[2]	6.4	4.4	7.7	8.4	5.5	7.6
National saving/GDP[1]	22.9	24.3	21.7	24.0	30.3	34.3
Private	22.8	22.4	21.0	24.4	26.0	27.1
Public	0.1	1.9	0.7	–0.4	4.3	7.2
Open unemployment	...	...	...	2.0	1.0	0.6
Total factor productivity[3]	–0.2	–0.8	2.6	–0.6	6.5	1.6
External debt/GDP	15.7	12.0	21.2	33.5	36.2	40.5
Debt-service ratio (in percent of exports of goods and nonfactor services)	7.4	7.8	14.4	23.4	17.7	11.8
Memorandum:						
Real GDP growth valued at PPP[4]	5.9	3.9	7.9	4.5	11.1	6.5

Sources: IMF, *International Financial Statistics* (various years); World Bank, *World Debt Tables* (various years); and Thai authorities.
[1] At current prices.
[2] Government and public enterprises.
[3] TFP is calculated as a residual after taking into account estimated contributions of capital and labor.
[4] The PPP estimates of GDP are from the Penn World Tables, Mark 5 (Summers and Heston, 1991).

lagged responses of the private sector to the exogenous shocks). However, the responses do give a broad indication of how the external sector adjustment was achieved.

Table 5 shows the magnitude of the shocks in percent of GDP and the responses of the economy, also as a ratio to GDP. Three distinct phases are discernible. First, between 1980 and 1982 the most significant outcome was a major reduction in import intensity, along with a modest improvement in export market shares. That real GDP growth was below trend during these years contributed to the decline in imports and to the improvement in the external current account, but this was much less important than the change in import intensity. Second, in 1983–86 the declining trend of import intensity was reversed. Third, during 1987–93 there were large increases in both export and import market shares.

Figure 4 depicts the growth in real domestic absorption (and its components) and net exports, and

Figure 3. Terms of Trade Movements
(Index, 1990 = 100)

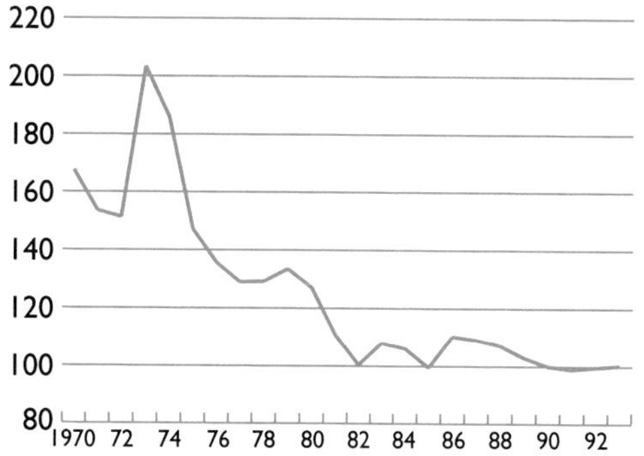

Source: International Monetary Fund, *International Financial Statistics* (various issues).

Table 5. Responses to Exogenous Shocks
(Cumulative effect; in percent of GDP unless otherwise noted)

Phase of Adjustment	Total Shocks[1]	Change in Export Market Share[2]	Change in Import Intensity[3]	Change in Imports Attributed to Deviations of Output from Trend[4]	Average Growth in Import Volume (in percent)	Average Growth in Export Volume (in percent)
1979–82	11.0	3.3	8.9	2.5	–2.0	5.7
1983–86	–3.8	0.8	–4.6	0.1	4.9	5.8
1987–93	2.7	17.5	–7.0	–1.9	19.6	18.3

Sources: IMF, *International Financial Statistics* (various years); and IMF staff estimates.

[1]Calculated as the sum of the terms of trade shock, the decline in export volumes owing to global recessions, and the interest rate shock. A positive value indicates an adverse shock.

[2]Calculated as deviation from ratios of exports/GDP projected by applying a constant income elasticity (estimated over the preceding five-year period) to the actual growth in partner-country demand. Positive values correspond to gains in market shares.

[3]Calculated as the deviation from ratio of imports/GDP projected by applying a constant income elasticity (estimated over the preceding five-year period) to actual GDP growth in Thailand. Negative values correspond to import intensification.

[4]Positive values imply import compression, which is calculated as the impact of deviations of GDP growth from a five-year moving-average trend, assuming an unchanged income elasticity of import demand.

the gap between actual and trend real GDP before, during, and after the adjustment phase.[11]

Notable points are the following. First, in the five years before the adjustment programs, consumption and investment by the public sector grew considerably more rapidly than that of their private sector counterparts. Second, during the adjustment period, there was a significant reduction in the growth of consumption and investment (especially public investment). Third, the growth in net exports during the adjustment period indicates that expenditure and production switching—primarily through a sharp reduction in imports and moderate growth in exports—played an important role in Thailand's adjustment. Fourth, the growth in real absorption in the postadjustment phase was unprecedented, with the largest contribution being made by private investment. Gross investment as a share of GDP rose by over 15 percentage points between 1986 and 1993; indeed, national saving also rose during this period, and the share of consumption in GDP declined markedly. Fifth, the output gap measure suggests that output was significantly below potential during

the entire adjustment period and that it was not until 1987 that output growth recovered to potential.

Linking Outcomes to Policies

What role did macroeconomic and structural policies play in generating the outcomes described above? With regard to responses to the first set of shocks, how was the decline in import intensity in the 1980–82 period achieved? Despite a nominal devaluation of about 9 percent in 1981, the real effective exchange rate (Figure 5) steadily appreciated between 1979 and 1984 as the U.S. dollar strengthened against other currencies. Movements in the real effective exchange rate thus do not appear to be consistent with a decline in import intensity. The answer appears to lie in three factors. First, despite the real appreciation of the baht, competitiveness as measured by relative unit labor costs was broadly unchanged during this period (see Figure 5).[12] Closer examination of underlying trends reveals that although unit labor costs rose in Thailand, the increases were much smaller than in some of its major trading partners, particularly in the United States.

---

[11]Trend output was calculated using the Hodrick-Prescott filter, a univariate trend-extraction algorithm that is based on actual real GDP. The filter calculates trend GDP by minimizing the variation of actual GDP around a trend, subject to certain assumptions about the variance of the cyclical component relative to that of the trend component.

---

[12]Unit labor costs in the manufacturing sector in Thailand were compared with a trade-weighted average of unit labor costs in the United States, United Kingdom, Germany, France, the Netherlands, Hong Kong, Singapore, Korea, Taiwan Province of China, and Malaysia.

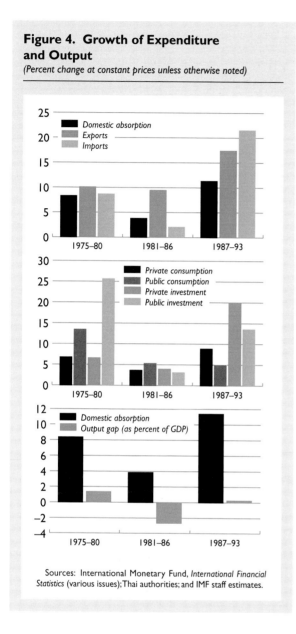

Figure 4. Growth of Expenditure and Output
(Percent change at constant prices unless otherwise noted)

Sources: International Monetary Fund, *International Financial Statistics* (various issues); Thai authorities; and IMF staff estimates.

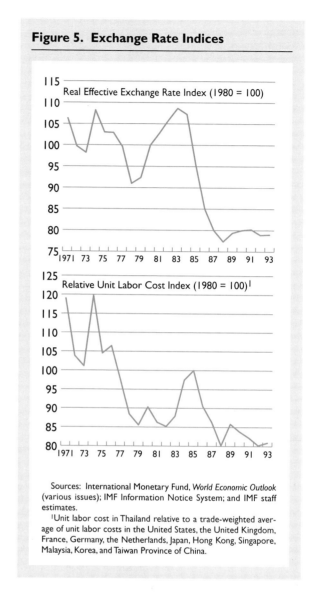

Figure 5. Exchange Rate Indices

Sources: International Monetary Fund, *World Economic Outlook* (various issues); IMF Information Notice System; and IMF staff estimates.

¹Unit labor cost in Thailand relative to a trade-weighted average of unit labor costs in the United States, the United Kingdom, France, Germany, the Netherlands, Japan, Hong Kong, Singapore, Malaysia, Korea, and Taiwan Province of China.

Second, a change in the orientation of trade and industrial policy in favor of less import-intensive sectors occurred, despite the stated objective of trade reforms in this period to move away from the previous emphasis on import substitution. At first, in addition to the devaluation in 1981, export taxes were reduced, and an attempt was made to rationalize tariffs. However, budgetary problems quickly led to the imposition of import surcharges. Less import-intensive sectors such as agriculture and agroprocessing experienced an increase in the effective rate of protection (see Section VII). Third, expenditure reduction during this period was concentrated mainly in the import-intensive categories, primarily capital expenditures of the government and public enterprises.

Thus, the appreciation of the baht combined with the increase in protection led to "inward-oriented" adjustment during this period. This mix of policies, which contributed to the tapering off of the export expansion, appears to have been detrimental to the recovery in growth, which remained below trend until 1986–87.

What factors accounted for the shift, in 1986–87, in the pattern of external adjustment to one driven almost entirely by increases in export market shares? A significant change in the policy mix occurred, starting with the nominal devaluation of the baht vis-à-vis the U.S. dollar in late 1984. The baht was devalued by nearly 15 percent in nominal terms just ahead of the Plaza Accord, and it subsequently was pegged to an undisclosed basket of currencies. As the dollar fell against the yen in the second half of the 1980s, the weight of the dollar in the basket was raised so that a significant nominal devaluation took place vis-à-vis the yen and some other East Asian currencies.

A dramatic reversal took place in the trend in the real effective exchange rate as the nominal devaluation was translated into a significant and sustained real effective depreciation, owing mainly to the support of conservative financial policies that kept inflation in check. The other important element of the shift in the policy mix was the massive tightening of fiscal policy, which served to accommodate the surge in export-oriented domestic and foreign-financed private investment. Also, export taxation was eliminated, and industrial policies were reoriented to take a proactive approach to export promotion, mainly through the provision of various tax incentives. The presence of generally flexible labor markets and the absence of systematic wage-price inertia were instrumental in generating the resource shifts necessary to produce the impressive supply response of the second half of the 1980s.

Although there was a marked slowdown in output growth in the immediate aftermath of the devaluation, in part owing to a decline in business confidence as banks and firms that had borrowed heavily from abroad suffered large losses when the currency was devalued, output growth rebounded sharply and relatively quickly. By 1987, the output gap had turned positive again. After a short lag following the devaluation, exports responded vigorously; since 1986, export volume growth averaged almost 18 percent annually.

The second shock that Thailand faced was the sharp increase in capital inflows beginning in 1987–88.[13] Most of these inflows were attributable to foreign direct investment. The major causes for the inflows were the sharp depreciation of the baht vis-à-vis the currencies of several large East Asian economies and rising labor costs in these economies, which led, in turn, to considerable relocation of production to Thailand.[14] For the most part, the surge in capital inflows was perceived by the authorities as a response to fundamental changes in the attractiveness of Thailand to foreign investors. However, the threat of overheating was also a major concern. The policy responses of the Thai authorities to these inflows reflected these concerns.

The first line of defense was the tightening of fiscal policy, a policy choice that was reinforced as the durability of the inflows and their impact on investment and growth became clear. Other policy responses included effective sterilization of monetary impulses and the maintenance of a generally tight monetary policy stance; selective reduction of trade barriers, especially beginning in 1991; liberalization of capital outflows, also since 1991; reductions of direct controls on interest rates and credit, since 1990; and the reimposition of a withholding tax on foreign borrowing. Together, these measures helped the authorities to accommodate the surge in capital inflows without a significant acceleration in inflation, and the increase in the investment rate contributed to the marked acceleration in growth.[15]

Investment and Saving

Figure 6 outlines the evolution of saving-investment balances since the early 1970s. Consumption smoothing in response to the first oil price shock led to a decline in saving while investment levels were maintained virtually unchanged. Widening current account imbalances mirrored the resulting saving-investment gap. The response to the second oil price shock was similar—investment rates were maintained largely unchanged in the early 1980s, and the saving rate, especially that of the private sector, again declined. The resulting external imbalances increasingly became a concern to the authorities. In response, the renewed macroeconomic adjustment efforts of 1984/85 had fiscal consolidation as their centerpiece. Public sector saving began its striking growth, and, with the marked increase in output growth that also occurred during this period, private saving and investment rates rose dramatically—reaching 25 percent and 32 percent of GDP, respectively, by the early 1990s.

The behavior of private investment in Thailand since the mid-1980s prompts two questions. First, why was the initial decline in investment in the post-stabilization period so short-lived, in contrast to the experience of many developing countries? Second, what factors accounted for the remarkable surge in investment in the second half of the 1980s?

Econometric evidence presented in the appendix suggests that the decline in private investment in the mid-1980s was attributable to high real interest rates and tight credit conditions. As regards the surge in private investment in the second half of the 1980s, although it can be ascribed in part to fortuitous ex-

[13]Total long- and short-term inflows averaged about 10 percent of GDP annually between 1987–88 and 1993.

[14]Another factor was rising protectionist pressures between the United States and Japan. By the mid-1980s, such pressures, in conjunction with the appreciation of the yen, led to production shifting from Japan to Thailand, a country with which Japan has had long-standing close cultural and business ties.

[15]Thailand's policy response to the surge in capital inflows has been discussed in more detail in Bercuson and Koenig (1993) and in Schadler and others (1993).

Figure 6. Saving and Investment
(In percent of GDP at current prices)

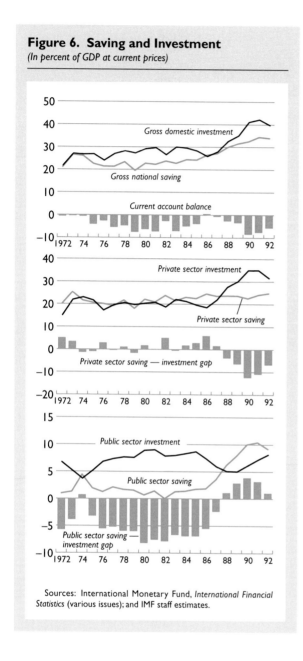

Sources: International Monetary Fund, *International Financial Statistics* (various issues); and IMF staff estimates.

in a marked improvement in competitiveness. Moreover, flexible labor markets (judged in terms of real wage flexibility and labor mobility) were an important factor underlying the developments in relative unit labor costs and, in turn, the favorable path of investment in both the stabilization period and beyond. The data also suggest that there is substitutability between public and private investment in Thailand, at least in the short term. A key implication of this result is that the surge in private investment could be accommodated without a significant acceleration in inflation because of the simultaneous rationalization and reduction of public expenditure, including on investment, that began in the late 1980s. However, the costs of this conservative public investment policy stance became increasingly apparent in the early 1990s, when severe infrastructure bottlenecks emerged.

Finally and crucially, overall macroeconomic stability, combined with the consistently pro-business orientation of the government, resulted in relatively low policy uncertainty and has proven to be conducive to private investment, both domestic and foreign. The absence of a significant and prolonged decline in investment during and after the stabilization phase is, in large part, attributable to these characteristics of economic policies as well as to the existence of a well-developed and dynamic private sector.

As regards the behavior of saving, it is clear that the increase in national saving (as well as the large private capital inflows) played a key role by providing noninflationary financing for the investment boom. Econometric evidence on the determinants of saving in Thailand, from internal IMF staff studies, suggests that three factors account for the bulk of the increase in the saving rate. First, the strong increase in public saving that accompanied the fiscal consolidation of the late 1980s is estimated to have increased the gross national saving rate by over 6 percentage points. The evidence also indicates that, contrary to the general experience in most developing countries, changes in public saving did not have a significant offsetting impact on private saving. Second, the sustained rapid growth in private disposable incomes was instrumental in raising the rate of private saving. Finally, substantial demographic changes, reflected in the increase in the working-age population, contributed in important ways to the sharp rise in saving.

ogenous developments—such as the currency realignments and rising labor costs in several East Asian countries—policy-related factors contributed significantly. The devaluation of the baht, buttressed by the conservative monetary policy stance, resulted

IV   Fiscal Policy

How did fiscal policy contribute to the result that the slowdown in growth during the adjustment period was relatively modest and was followed by a shift to a markedly higher growth path? Two aspects of the fiscal adjustment are considered here: its contribution to demand management and its effects on the medium-term debt dynamics of the public sector.

There was actually no sustained reduction in the fiscal deficit during most of the "adjustment" phase of the first half of the 1980s (Table 6). A number of new tax measures were introduced, and efforts were made to improve tax administration and collection. Nevertheless, the sluggishness in growth and the slowdown in world demand limited the initial increases in revenue from these measures. At the same time, efforts to contain the growth of noninterest current expenditure proved largely unsuccessful; as external debt accumulated, interest payments on public debt rose sharply. Moreover, attempts to reduce the public sector deficit proved inadequate, in large part owing to a chronic tendency to overestimate revenues. Combined with the difficulty of achieving midyear reductions in expenditures from their budgeted levels, this tendency led to deficits that were persistently larger than targeted. Figure 7, which plots programmed (as indicated in the first programs of each of the stand-by arrangements with the IMF) and actual budget deficits during the adjustment period, confirms this tendency.

In contrast, there was a sharp fiscal adjustment in the second half of the 1980s, a period that coincided with the surge in private investment and exports. Part of the deficit reduction stemmed from strong revenue growth as a result of the improved elasticity of the tax system, but the bulk of the adjustment came from discretionary reductions in, and a rationalization of, expenditures. In particular, capital spending fell in nominal terms, while the growth in current expenditure was limited. These measures were supported by a move toward more conservative budgetary procedures, especially in forecasting revenues, in 1985/86. This change in procedures reinforced the institutional bias toward conservative fiscal policies that is imparted by the Budget Law, which limits the planned government budget deficit each year to no more than 20 percent of planned expenditures plus 80 percent of scheduled amortization payments on government debt.

Capital spending rebounded in the 1990s, driven by an urgent need to increase infrastructure spending to relieve severe bottlenecks that had developed in the Bangkok area. Nevertheless, the buoyancy of revenues in response to the continued strong growth in output, as well as a continued decline in current spending as a share of GDP, resulted in a sharp rise in public saving and in growing fiscal surpluses.

Fiscal Impulse and the Stance of Fiscal Policy

It is difficult to analyze the effects of fiscal policy on aggregate demand in the absence of a full model, but some simple fiscal impulse measures do give some broad indication of the direction and magnitude of the likely effects. Table 7 presents the average annual fiscal impulse in the preadjustment, adjustment, and postadjustment periods.[16] The results suggest that fiscal policy provided a strong stimulus to demand during the "preadjustment" period. Fiscal policy was considerably less expansionary during the "adjustment" period; as for its impact on aggregate demand, it was broadly neutral.

---

[16]The fiscal impulse measure used here is similar to that used in the IMF's *World Economic Outlook* (see Heller, Haas, and Mansur, 1986). It is calculated by separating the actual budget balance into two components: a cyclically neutral component and a fiscal stance component. The cyclically neutral component is defined by assuming that government expenditures increase proportionately with trend nominal output and that government revenues increase proportionately with actual nominal output. The fiscal stance component—the difference between the cyclically neutral and the actual budget balance—then captures the full effect of automatic stabilizers and discretionary changes in fiscal policy. The fiscal impulse is the annual change in the fiscal stance measure, expressed as a share of GDP. A negative number would indicate a contractionary demand impulse emanating from fiscal policy, and a positive number would indicate an expansionary demand impulse.

Table 6. Overview of Fiscal Developments¹

	1975–1980	1981–86	1987–89	1990–93
	Annual average percent change			
Revenues	16.3	10.3	23.4	17.4
Current noninterest expenditure	23.0	8.9	7.6	17.2
Interest payments	21.3	24.4	8.1	–12.4
Capital expenditure	27.5	8.5	–1.8	38.1
	In percent of GDP			
Revenues	13.0	14.5	15.7	18.0
Current noninterest expenditure	11.2	12.8	10.2	9.5
Interest payments	1.2	2.5	2.6	1.4
Capital expenditure	4.1	4.1	2.8	3.3
Overall budget deficit	–3.3	–4.5	0.5	3.9

Source: IMF, *Government Finance Statistics Yearbook* (various years).
¹Based on the accounts of the central government.

However, it was not until 1986 that significant inroads were made in reducing the overall fiscal deficit. Fiscal policy during the postadjustment phase can be characterized as strongly countercyclical. Discretionary policy, particularly restraint on expenditures, had a large role to play in this outcome, but automatic stabilizers—notably the high income elasticity of taxes—also contributed. The countercyclical stance of fiscal policy was of criti-

cal importance in easing the pressures on demand in the face of the large capital inflows of the late 1980s and early 1990s, which generated a prolonged investment boom. Through its influences on both the level and composition of aggregate demand, the restrained fiscal stance helped to mitigate the upward pressures on the real exchange rate and thereby also helped to sustain the strong export growth (see Figure 4).

Issues in the Sustainability of Public Debt

Private sector assessments of the sustainability of fiscal policy can have an important effect on the response of private investment and saving. A major consideration in any assessment of sustainability is how the fiscal policy stance will affect the public sector debt burden. Figure 8 and Table 8 present the

Figure 7. Actual Versus Programmed Budget Balances
(In percent of GDP)

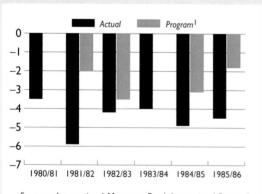

Sources: International Monetary Fund, *International Financial Statistics* (various issues); and IMF staff estimates.
¹"Program" refers to the budget balances programmed under the first program of each of the three IMF stand-by arrangements with Thailand during this period.

Table 7. Fiscal Impulse and Output Gaps
(In percent of GDP)

	1978–80	1981–86	1987–93
Average output gap	4.2	–2.7	0.3
Average fiscal impulse	1.3	0.2	–0.8

Sources: IMF staff estimates.

Table 8. Fiscal Sustainability
(In percent of GDP unless otherwise noted)

	1975–84 Average	1985	1986	1987	1988–90 Average	1991–93 Average
Total public debt	14.7	25.9	29.8	28.3	21.2	9.9
Domestic	10.8	17.1	19.9	19.1	14.6	6.3
Foreign	3.9	8.8	9.9	9.2	6.6	3.6
Share of external debt on concessional terms (in percent)	17.8	15.3	18.0	20.8	21.8	21.4
Share of external debt at variable interest rates (in percent)	51.5	49.8	46.0	42.0	49.0	56.3
External debt-service ratio	18.5	31.9	30.1	22.0	17.8	15.2
Seigniorage	1.2	0.6	0.8	1.2	1.5	1.1
Real interest rate on external debt (in percent a year)	4.2	5.7	5.1	4.3	4.1	3.7
Real interest rate on domestic debt (in percent a year)	4.5	11.1	9.3	7.3	6.5	8.0
Real GDP growth	6.7	5.3	6.6	9.4	11.6	8.2
Differential between interest rates and the growth rate $(r - n)$	-2.2	3.8	1.3	-2.8	-5.2	-1.6
Actual primary fiscal balance	-1.3	-1.3	-0.7	0.8	4.5	4.7
Sustainable primary balance	-1.5	0.4	-0.5	-2.0	-2.6	-1.3

Sources: IMF, *International Financial Statistics* and *Government Finance Statistics Yearbook* (various years); World Bank, *World Debt Tables* (various years); and IMF staff estimates.

results of some calculations of debt dynamics for Thailand based on the intertemporal budget constraint for the public sector. The actual primary fiscal balance at different stages in the adjustment process is compared with a "sustainable" position, defined as the primary balance needed to keep the ratio of public sector debt to GNP constant, on the assumption that the rate of inflation (which influences seigniorage) remains low and that the current interest rate on domestic debt is maintained.[17]

The results show that, throughout the period under consideration, there were few grounds for concern about the medium-term sustainability of Thailand's fiscal policy from the perspective of an ability to service the public debt in a manner that was consistent with low inflation.[18] Although during most of the adjustment period the actual primary balance was in excess of what can be deemed as "sustainable," a period of rising debt-to-GNP ratios may have been tolerable (albeit not strictly sustainable by the definition used here), given Thailand's low initial level of debt. In any event, the gap between actual and sustainable fiscal balances turned sharply positive by the end of the adjustment period and has remained so since then. Of course, this measure does not address the more fundamental judgment of whether a fiscal balance that is sustainable by the above criterion is also consistent with other macroeconomic objectives including the external current account balance. Moreover, it does not address the issue of the

[17]Using the approach set out in Anand and van Wijnbergen (1989), the budget constraint can be described as $\Delta b = (r - n)b + d - s$, where b represents the public debt-to-GDP ratio, d is the primary deficit as a share of GDP, s represents seigniorage revenues (including the inflation tax) as a share of GDP, r stands for the average real interest rate on debt, and n is the real GDP growth rate. Since the aim of the exercise is to assess whether fiscal policy was judged to be sustainable at the time of adjustment, rather than with the benefit of hindsight, the debt calculations are based on a three-year moving average of actual interest rates and growth rates. The calculations also assume, for each year's estimate, that the real exchange rate is expected to be constant.

[18]For the purposes of illustration, the sustainable fiscal balance was recalculated assuming that all external financing is on commercial terms. Given the relatively small share of external debt on concessional terms in Thailand, the impact of this assumption is marginal.

Figure 8. Actual and Sustainable Primary Balances
(In percent of GDP)

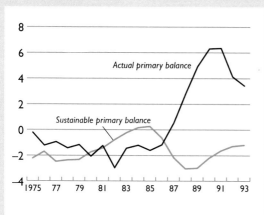

Sources: International Monetary Fund, *Government Finance Statistics Yearbook* (various issues); World Bank, *World Debt Tables* (various issues); and IMF staff estimates.

likely permanence of fiscal measures used to obtain a sustainable balance.

Key Lessons

The central messages that emerge from this discussion are, first, that fiscal policy was broadly neutral with respect to its impact on aggregate demand during most of the adjustment phase of the early 1980s. This is consistent with the finding in the next section that the brunt of adjustment was borne by monetary policy, as evidenced by the sharp increase in real lending rates. Second, the major fiscal correction actually took place in the postadjustment period and was an important factor in creating room for the surge in private investment and exports. Third, the authorities were able to implement what turned out to be a broadly countercyclical fiscal policy over these two periods, in part because the public (and external) debt situation remained manageable and did not require a sharp fiscal correction to reestablish credibility in terms of its consistency with the objective of low inflation.

V Monetary Policy

What role did monetary policy play in the adjustment process in Thailand, and what were the consequences for investment and output? In view of the fixed exchange rate and the relatively open capital account, one must first examine the scope for discretionary monetary policy. Empirical evidence suggests that there was some scope for independent monetary actions, especially in the short run, although the financial sector reforms that were implemented in the early 1990s have narrowed that ability.[19]

Monetary Conditions

How tight were monetary conditions during the adjustment period of the early 1980s? Relevant indicators include the level of real interest rates, movements in the differential vis-à-vis foreign interest rates, changes in the real rate of growth of private sector credit, and changes in the growth of reserve money. Most of the adjustment period witnessed historically high real interest rates, which peaked in 1984–85 (Figure 9). Real interest rates were consistently higher than growth rates of actual and potential real GDP—the latter is relevant because, over the long run, it should be related to the rate of return on investment. Real interest rates that are significantly and consistently above the long-run growth rate can be seen as indicative of, among other things, excessively tight monetary conditions. Moreover, Figure 9 shows that the gap between domestic and foreign real interest rates widened during this period.

As regards the growth rates of credit variables, private sector credit growth in real terms declined sharply during the adjustment period. Likewise, the

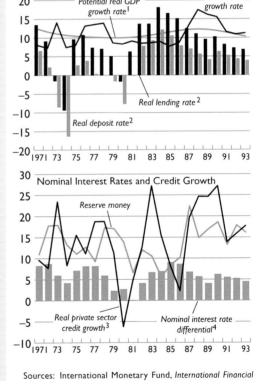

Figure 9. Interest Rates and Growth Rates
(In percent)

Sources: International Monetary Fund, *International Financial Statistics* (various issues); and IMF staff estimates.
[1]Calculated using the Hodrick-Prescott filter procedure.
[2]Ex post real interest rates, adjusted for consumer price inflation.
[3]Deflated by the consumer price index.
[4]Differential between Thai lending rates and the U.S. prime lending rate.

---

[19]See Robinson, Byeon, and Teja (1991). The Thai capital account has been quite open, especially for inflows, with a few important limitations. First, for prudential reasons, limits are imposed on the open foreign exchange position of commercial banks. Second, banks are not allowed to make foreign-currency-denominated loans, and, until the early 1990s, residents were not permitted to hold foreign currency deposits at domestic banks. Third, until the elimination in 1990 and 1992 of ceilings on interest rates, both lending and deposit rates were subject to regulatory ceilings. Various controls on capital outflows limited the extent of arbitrage in response to interest rate differentials. Fourth, foreign borrowing is subject to a withholding tax at rates that are varied from time to time to regulate capital inflows.

growth rate of reserve money fell from an annual average of 16 percent in 1978–80 to below 9 percent in 1981–86 before increasing sharply to an average of over 17 percent in the 1987–93 period. Thus, all indicators suggest that monetary conditions were tight, especially in the later years of the adjustment period. Indeed, since fiscal policy was not contractionary for most of this period, tight monetary conditions appear to have been an important policy factor accounting for the slowdown in aggregate demand and the emergence of an output "gap" in this period (see Figure 4). However, it is difficult to disentangle the effect of tight credit conditions from the impact on output growth of the slump in commodity prices and the global recession, which depressed export receipts, business sentiments, and domestic demand.

Figure 10 plots programmed and actual growth rates of total domestic credit and private sector credit during the adjustment period. For total credit growth, actual credit growth slightly exceeded programmed credit growth during the early years of adjustment. The 1985/86 adjustment program called for continued tight credit conditions to contain the inflationary impact of the devaluation. In real terms, credit was to grow by less than 10 percent. In the event, actual credit growth turned out to be considerably slower than programmed, largely as a consequence of the stagnation in private domestic demand.

Key Lessons

On the basis of empirical estimates of the determinants of private investment (see the appendix), the high real lending interest rates during this period did restrain investment growth. At the same time, however, the conservative stance of monetary policy helped to translate the nominal devaluation of 1984 into a sustained real depreciation, thereby laying the foundation for the marked success of expenditure-switching policies that was crucial to Thailand's rapid recovery after stabilization.

More fundamentally, an important lesson from the conduct of monetary policy in Thailand concerns the benefits that accrue from long-run monetary discipline and the high degree of policy credibility asso-

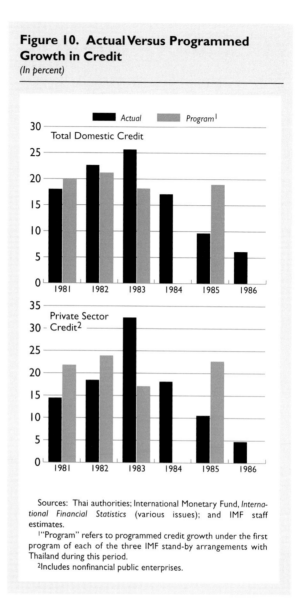

Figure 10. Actual Versus Programmed Growth in Credit
(In percent)

Sources: Thai authorities; International Monetary Fund, *International Financial Statistics* (various issues); and IMF staff estimates.
[1]"Program" refers to programmed credit growth under the first program of each of the three IMF stand-by arrangements with Thailand during this period.
[2]Includes nonfinancial public enterprises.

ciated with it. These attributes allowed a quick reversal of inflation and the rapid shift in resources toward the traded-goods sector in the mid- to late 1980s to be achieved without a recession.

VI   Labor Markets

This section examines the role of labor markets in the adjustment process. In particular, it examines the role of labor market and wage flexibility in bringing about the rapid resource reallocation necessitated by the shocks and the policy response of the late 1970s and early 1980s.

Institutional Characteristics

Characteristics of labor markets in developing countries can have a major impact on the transmission of shocks and policies to real economic activity. *Labor market segmentation*—between traditional and modern sectors, urban and rural labor markets, or skilled and unskilled members of the labor force—restricts labor mobility and can result in persistent wage differentials, which in turn can deter the efficient reallocation of resources in response to shocks and policy changes. *Wage flexibility* may be limited by a variety of labor market regulations such as minimum wage laws or by other factors such as powerful trade unions. Moreover, *public sector employment and wage policies* are often slow to adjust to changing economic conditions; the latter can have a considerable "leverage" effect on private sector wages.

Few of these features appear to be of major importance in the case of Thailand. A study by Bertrand and Squire (1980) found that labor market segmentation was small; urban labor markets, especially those in the Bangkok metropolitan area, were in general characterized by low unemployment rates and appeared to be well integrated with rural labor markets. The active urban informal sector provided employment at wages that were not far below those in the formal sector.[20]

Labor union activity in Thailand is limited; although minimum wage legislation exists, it is effective only in the public sector and in some large private sector firms, which employ a small fraction of the workforce. According to a survey conducted in 1986, less than one third of all enterprises in operation paid the minimum wage or higher, implying that fewer than half of all unskilled workers were being paid the minimum wage.[21] Moreover, the legislated real minimum wages declined through most of the period under consideration. The majority of employment occurs in agriculture, small private firms in the manufacturing sector, and the service sector, where labor markets appear to be competitive and wages flexible.

Finally, public sector employment, including the civil service and state enterprises, is relatively small. It grew quite rapidly during the expansionary phase of the late 1970s, rising from a little over 4 percent of the labor force to over 7 percent in only a few years, but its share in the labor force has remained broadly unchanged since then. Public sector employment accounts for about a fourth of all formal sector employment. The answer is not clear whether wages in the public sector contribute to wage pressures in the rest of the formal sector. On the one hand, civil service compensation and wages in state enterprises have tended to be considerably lower than those in the private sector. On the other hand, the differential between average private and public sector wages has tended to be maintained, suggesting that public sector wage adjustments could put pressure on wages in the rest of the formal sector.

Trends in Employment and Unemployment

Table 9 presents trends in employment in the agricultural and manufacturing sectors during the

---

[20]Although the evidence is fragmentary and somewhat outdated, Bertrand and Squire's analysis suggests that there is little open unemployment in rural Thailand; that wage differentials between agriculture and manufacturing do not appear to be out of line with productivity differentials; that minimum wages in the formal sector and wages of unskilled labor in certain manufacturing activities are not significantly different from each other and that they tend to move together over time; and that participation rates are high, and unemployment rates low, among migrant labor moving into the urban labor market.

---

[21]Despite the limited effective coverage of minimum wages, revisions to the minimum wage do tend to raise the entire salary structure of the formal sector. However, as will be seen below, wage increases have thus far not generally been out of line with productivity developments, particularly in the manufacturing sector. The potential distortions that can arise from such regulations do not appear to have been relevant in Thailand during the period under study.

Table 9. Employment Trends
(Percent Change)

	1975–80	1981–86	1987–93
Agriculture	...	2.1	2.0
Manufacturing	2.2	4.8	7.7

Sources: Thai authorities.

Figure 11. Productivity, Real Wages, and Wage Gaps

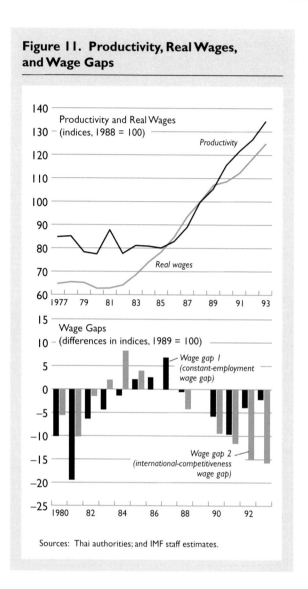

Sources: Thai authorities; and IMF staff estimates.

period under consideration. A striking feature of the trends is the increase in the growth rate of manufacturing employment in the postadjustment period, which suggests that labor market flexibility did permit significant resource allocation in response to the adjustment policies.

Data on unemployment in Thailand are fragmentary, and what information is available is fraught with problems, including significant changes in definitions during the period under consideration. Even so, certain clear trends are discernible in open unemployment rates.[22] The unemployment rate has remained small but has broadly paralleled movements in the output "gap" (Table 10). It rose moderately during the adjustment phase, peaking at 2½ percent in 1984–85, before declining sharply to an average of less than 1 percent in the postadjustment period. The absence of severe distortions in labor markets, as well as the behavior of real wages (discussed below), contributed toward keeping the impact of adjustment policies on unemployment small.

Flexibility of Real Wages

Was there flexibility in real wages during the adjustment period—in particular, were movements in real wages consistent with the necessary adjustment in resource allocation? One measure of flexibility is the extent to which real wages have remained in line with the level that would be warranted by high-employment considerations. Another is the extent to which real wages remained in line with the level that would be warranted from the perspective of maintaining international competitiveness. This second measure is of particular importance for relatively

open economies. Specifically, the issue is whether real wage movements helped to preserve—or even augment—international competitiveness in response to external shocks.

Table 10. Output Gap and Unemployment

	1973–80	1981–86	1987–93
Output gap (in percent of GDP)	1.4	−2.7	0.3
Unemployment (in percent of labor force)	...	2.0	0.8

Sources: Thai authorities; and IMF staff estimates.

[22]Open unemployment is defined to include those who were looking for work and those who were available and willing to work.

Table 11. Actual and "Warranted" Real Consumption Wages in the Manufacturing Sector
(Percent change unless otherwise noted)

	Productivity Growth	Unit Labor Costs in Partner Countries	Warranted Real Wages 1[1]	Warranted Real Wages 2[2]	Actual Real Wages	Wage Gap 1[3]	Wage Gap 2[4]
1975–80	9.3	9.7	8.2	10.0	1.3	−11.3	−10.9
1981–83	2.1	0.3	0.6	−0.8	3.1	−10.0	−3.2
1981	13.3	0.1	13.7	7.3	0.2	−19.4	−10.2
1982	−11.5	0.5	−15.1	−10.8	2.1	−6.3	−1.5
1983	4.4	0.4	3.2	1.1	6.9	−4.3	2.0
1984–86	0.7	4.9	3.9	8.8	7.3	1.2	4.0
1984	−0.3	−3.3	3.1	−1.7	8.0	−1.3	8.2
1985	−0.9	2.0	0.7	13.5	5.8	2.2	4.0
1986	3.4	16.1	7.9	14.5	8.2	2.7	—
1987–93	7.2	5.4	6.6	7.6	5.7	−2.1	−8.0

Sources: IMF, World Economic Outlook database; Thai authorities; and IMF staff estimates.
[1]Changes in warranted wage are given by changes in productivity plus the change in the price of output relative to the consumer price index.
[2]Changes in warranted wages are given by changes in productivity adjusted for changes in the real exchange rate and changes in unit labor costs in partner countries.
[3]Difference between an index of actual wages and one of warranted wages measured as in footnote 1. Indices are based in 1989.
[4]Difference between an index of actual wages and one of warranted wages measured as in footnote 2. Indices are based in 1989.

Two indicators—both quantifying the discrepancy ("wage gap") between the actual wage and estimates of the "warranted" real wage on the basis of the above two considerations—were used to evaluate the question. The first measure of warranted real wages was estimated under the assumption that labor's share in value added is constant, implying an unchanged level of employment over time.[23] The implication of assuming a constant wage share would be that the growth in real consumption wages—measured in terms of purchasing power over consumption goods—should correspond to productivity increases adjusted for changes in output prices relative to consumption prices.[24] The second measure of warranted wages was estimated by comparing the behavior of productivity and exchange rates with that of unit labor costs in trading-partner countries.[25]

The evolution of real wages and labor productivity in the manufacturing sector is shown in Figure 11. Real wages declined moderately in the periods of the two oil price shocks, and productivity outpaced real wages for most of the 1970s. During the adjustment period (1980–86), however, real wage growth generally exceeded productivity growth. This development appears to be partly attributable to increases in public sector wages in the early 1980s. Since 1987, real wage growth has been more or less in line with productivity growth.

For the two measures of the wage gap, Table 11 presents the growth of actual and warranted wages on the basis of the two approaches, and Figure 11 plots the wage gaps. The wage gaps were calculated using 1989 as a base year—the potential output measures discussed earlier suggest that output was near capacity in 1989.[26] The magnitude of the wage gaps

---

[23]Bruno (1985) and Bruno and Sachs (1985) calculated wage gap measures by assuming that the underlying production technology is Cobb-Douglas in nature, with unitary elasticity of substitution between capital and labor. Under these assumptions, the issue of estimating the warranted wage is one of calculating average productivity at full employment. In contrast, the measure used here does not necessarily imply that the absence of a wage gap is appropriate from the point of view of *full* employment, only unchanged employment.

[24]The change in warranted wages is given by $\Delta (W/P_c) = \Delta (\text{Productivity}) + \Delta (P_m/P_c)$, where W is the nominal wage, P_c is the consumer price index, and P_m is the output deflator.

[25]It is given by

$$\Delta (W/P_c) \leq \Delta (ULC(\$)^*) + \Delta (\text{Productivity}) + \Delta (\text{Nominal exchange rate}) - \Delta (P_c).$$

[26]Wage gap measures can be strongly influenced by the choice of the base year; however, experiments with alternative base years were chosen in the postadjustment period and yielded similar measures of the wage gap.

was different using the two indicators, but the trends were similar.

In particular, during the late 1970s, actual wage growth was considerably below warranted wage growth, and wage gaps were substantially negative. During the first half of the adjustment period (1981–83), the wage gaps remained negative even as actual wage growth began to outpace that of warranted wages. By the second half of the adjustment period (1984–86), actual wage growth outstripped productivity growth by a wide margin, and wage gaps turned positive. The sustained real depreciation of the baht—owing to the nominal devaluation in late 1984, conservative financial policies and the continued depreciation of the U.S. dollar, and the pick-up in productivity growth beginning in 1986,

together with the rise in unit labor costs in trading partner countries—contributed to the reversal of these developments. Actual wage growth once again fell below that of warranted wages; wage gaps were negative during the entire postadjustment period.

The general conclusion of this analysis is that adjustment policies, together with the absence of systemic wage-price inertia, strong underlying productivity growth, and the track record of low inflation and inflationary expectations succeeded, albeit with some delay, in bringing about the necessary adjustment in real wages. In turn, this helped to contain the real costs of stabilization, in terms of a prolonged slowdown in output growth or an investment pause or both, and thereby set the stage for a rapid transition to a higher growth path.

VII Structural Reforms

This section focuses on the role that structural reforms have played in generating Thailand's sustained, rapid economic growth during the past two decades. At the outset, it should be noted that the difficulty of deriving simple quantitative measures to summarize the complex nature of structural reforms makes it equally difficult to identify statistically robust relationships between growth and structural policies. Nevertheless, the weight of the empirical evidence to date supports the conclusion that reforms designed to reduce allocative distortions have had a positive impact on the level and efficiency of capital formation and on growth.

The analytical basis for comparing sequences for removing structural distortions in a second-best world is limited, but the experiences of many developing countries do suggest a few general lessons.[27] First, there is broad consensus that, although it may not be a precondition for the initiation of reforms, structural adjustment without macroeconomic stability has typically not been successful in eliciting significant supply responses. Second, reforms must reach a critical mass to be effective. Marginal reductions in large distortions are not effective in increasing growth. Third, reforms that take a long time to put in place, such as institutional and regulatory improvements, should begin at an early stage of the adjustment process. Fourth, with regard to trade reforms, programs that begin with a substantial initial effort—involving the early elimination of quantitative restrictions and major tariff reductions—typically prove more successful in increasing growth. In addition, tariff reform is more likely to be sustained if it is supported by domestic tax reforms and, more generally, fiscal restructuring. Fifth, severe financial repression is inimical to the level and efficiency of investment and to growth, and it should be eliminated as rapidly as possible. Sixth, the primary objective of public enterprise reforms should be to improve efficiency, and this objective should not be overshadowed by the goal of generating (onetime) increases in fiscal receipts.

The story of structural reform in Thailand is very much one of *gradual changes* in a system that, in most cases, began with *relatively small distortions*. In some respects Thailand's structural reform efforts conformed with "best practices," while in others they did not. The almost uninterrupted maintenance of *macroeconomic stability* helped to offset the effects of the slow progress with structural adjustment. Moreover, the authorities generally took a *pragmatic approach* to structural reforms—when specific problems arose or when the effect of distortions became particularly acute, steps were taken to redress them quickly.

Financial Sector

The Thai financial system at the beginning of the 1970s was, in many ways, similar to that in many developing countries. The financial system was dominated by a small number of commercial banks with a high degree of concentration of ownership, and foreign banks played only a limited role. Interest rates on lending and deposits were subject to ceilings. Selective credit programs were used to allocate credit to "priority" sectors, the market for long-term capital was not well developed, and informal credit markets existed. Although the capital account was relatively open, especially for inflows, capital outflows were closely controlled. Banks were required to hold a certain proportion of their deposit liabilities in the form of government securities, but interest rates paid on government debt were positive in real terms.

Before the early 1990s, financial reforms in Thailand were not implemented according to any comprehensive blueprint, but rather in response to specific problems or circumstances. For example, during the first half of the 1980s there was a string of financial crises stemming from failures of finance companies and banks. Steps were then taken to strengthen bank supervision and deal more decisively with weak financial institutions. Likewise, the authorities recognized that interest rate ceilings and limits on capital outflows had become increasingly

---

[27]Lessons from various studies of adjustment programs are summarized in Appendix I of Goldsbrough and others (1996).

inconsistent with the rapid industrialization of the Thai economy. Thus, in the early 1990s, interest rate ceilings were lifted on a range of deposits, domestic banks were allowed to offer foreign currency deposit accounts, and capital outflows were substantially liberalized. However, the early 1990s saw a marked shift in the financial sector reform strategy toward a more coordinated and comprehensive package of reforms. Further liberalization took place in 1992 with the elimination of ceilings on lending interest rates.

Despite the lack of a comprehensive approach during most of the period, the indicators of financial sector development shown in Figure 12 suggest that initial distortions were not severe and that considerable financial sector development has taken place over the period under study. Real interest rates remained positive through most of the period, despite ceilings on nominal rates, suggesting that financial repression was not significant. The spread between deposit and lending rates was quite wide during most of the period but remained stable.[28] Since the early 1990s, this spread has narrowed significantly. The depth of the financial sector—proxied by the ratio of broad money to GDP—has risen steadily over this period and reached over 70 percent by 1992–93. The private sector's share of total credit has also risen, particularly since the second half of the 1980s, reflecting the decline in the government's claim on financial resources as a result of fiscal adjustment. On balance, the Thai financial system has been conducive to efficient financial intermediation and has supported the rapid growth in private investment in recent years.

Trade Reform

The Thai economy has traditionally been outward oriented; at the same time, however, there has been a fair degree of government intervention in the trade system. The main instrument of intervention has been tariffs.[29] The system of protection was biased against the agricultural sector and agro-based and labor-intensive manufacturing, and toward mostly capital-intensive import-substituting industries (au-

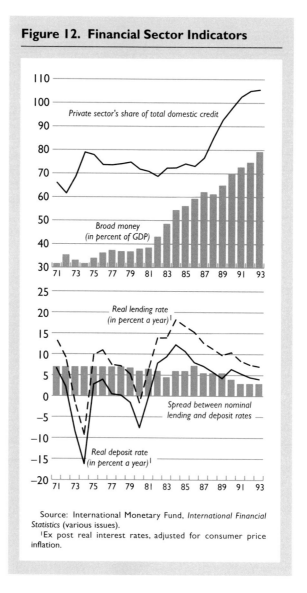

Figure 12. Financial Sector Indicators

Source: International Monetary Fund, *International Financial Statistics* (various issues).
[1] Ex post real interest rates, adjusted for consumer price inflation.

tomobiles and pharmaceuticals). The labor-intensive textile industry was also heavily protected.

Recent studies by Bhattacharya and Linn (1988) and Dean, Desai, and Riedel (1994) of the protection systems of East Asian countries found that Thailand's average nominal tariff rates were among the highest in the group, but that the coverage of nontariff barriers was relatively low. The studies conclude that the protection system in Thailand in the mid-1980s was broadly comparable to that in the Philippines and Korea.

Table 12 presents data on overall tariff rates and effective protection by sector and shows that little progress was made during the 1980s to reduce tariff protection. In part because of fiscal constraints and the need for revenues, only minor tariff reductions were implemented during this period (Figure 13).

---

[28]The spread between deposit and lending rates in Thailand, before 1990, averaged about 6.5 percentage points, compared with 1–2 percentage points in Malaysia and Korea, 3–4 percentage points in Indonesia and Singapore, and 5–6 percentage points in Sri Lanka and the Philippines.

[29]Although quantitative restrictions—including bans on automobile imports, and the application of domestic content rules—were used (especially during the 1970s), the coverage of quantitative restrictions has generally been relatively low—less than 5 percent of tariff lines—and has remained stable during the period under consideration.

Table 12. Tariffs and Effective Protection
(In percent)

	September 1981	March 1983	November 1984	April 1985	January 1988	1993
Nominal tariffs						
Unweighted average	31.0	32.6	29.9	33.8	...	30.2
Standard deviation	30.1	28.6	26.3	27.3	...	...
Weighted by import value						
Total	14.3	16.2	15.3	18.5	12.0	10.0
Consumer goods	25.0	22.6	20.7	24.8	...	16.0
Intermediate goods	13.2	15.7	14.5	14.1	...	8.1
Automotive goods	36.5	40.4	41.3	63.0	...	28.1
Capital goods	14.1	18.0	17.4	22.3	...	6.9
Raw materials	2.3	3.2	2.9	5.1	...	6.3
Effective rates of protection						
Unweighted average	66.7	66.4	59.0	65.9	64.6	...
Standard deviation	140.2	140.4	131.3	132.0	131.4	...
Weighted average	27.9	27.9	25.5	30.0	29.7	...
Agriculture	10.9	11.3	11.0	13.2	13.1	...
Agroprocessing	24.7	30.3	28.7	32.8	32.9	...
Other manufacturing	53.6	50.2	44.5	51.9	51.2	...
Textile products	110.4	61.1	55.5	59.9	59.9	...
Chemicals	49.3	54.0	46.7	9.2	9.5	...
Consumer goods and motor vehicles	51.5	54.6	48.3	70.0	68.7	...

Sources: IMF, *International Financial Statistics* (various years); World Bank staff estimates; and IMF extimates.

From the early 1990s, however, as the fiscal position strengthened and as the accumulation of international reserves intensified, serious attempts began to reduce and rationalize tariffs. Import-weighted average import taxes declined from 14 percent in 1986 to below 10 percent in 1993. Moreover, significant progress has been made in export taxation, which was concentrated in the taxation of rice exports. More recently (in early 1995), a program was launched to introduce tariff reductions over the next two years, at the end of which the average (unweighted) nominal tariff would decline to about 17 percent.

Clearly, Thailand's trade reform program during most of the period under review did not follow "best practices." The program did not begin with a substantial initial effort, in part because weaknesses in public finances acted as a constraint to more rapid tariff reforms. However, the slow progress with trade reforms did not have a dampening effect on long-term growth in Thailand because the trade system was not, in the first instance, so distorted as to have resulted in serious disincentives to export activities. The lack of a black market premium on the baht, in addition to being a result of the relatively open capital account (particularly for inflows), can be seen as one indication of the low level of overall distortions in the system.

Public Enterprises

The importance of public enterprises in the Thai economy increased during the phase of public sector expansion in the late 1970s and early 1980s. The ratio of public enterprise revenues to GDP rose from about 10 percent of GDP in the early 1970s to almost 18 percent by the early 1980s; it has since fallen slightly. Public enterprise investment rose from 1.7 percent of GDP in 1970 to about 3.5 percent of GDP in the 1981–86 period. By the mid-1980s, public enterprises accounted for over 70 percent of total public sector investment and about two-thirds of public sector external debt. In 1995, total public enterprise assets stood at over 50 percent of GDP. Of the 57 public enterprises, the largest in terms of assets and employment are public utilities, transport and communications companies, financial institutions, the petroleum company, and nonprofit institutions. In 1993, public utilities accounted for 42 percent of public enterprise assets, 85 percent of public enterprise capital expenditures, and two-thirds of employment.

Figure 13. Trade Taxation and Openness

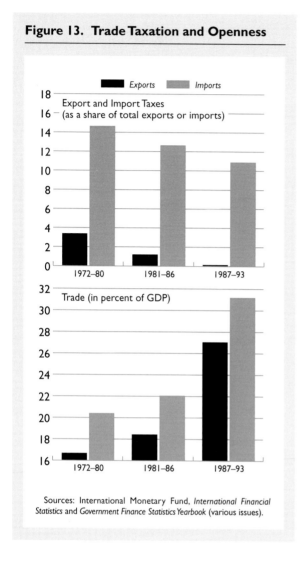

Sources: International Monetary Fund, *International Financial Statistics* and *Government Finance Statistics Yearbook* (various issues).

Compared with other developing countries, however, the sector plays a small role in the economy and has largely been restricted to the provision of transportation, communications, and public utilities.

For example, on average since the early 1970s, public enterprise investment has accounted for about 10 percent of total investment, compared with 20 percent in the Philippines, 33 percent in India, and nearly 40 percent in Turkey.

With the renewed commitment in the mid-1980s to streamlining the activities and increasing the efficiency of the public enterprise sector, public enterprise capital expenditures as a share of GDP declined to 2.7 percent between 1987 and 1989. However, little progress was made in privatization during this time. The large capital needs that have been projected for the coming years to address the serious infrastructure bottlenecks that have arisen in recent years have led the Thai authorities to seriously consider privatization, including in the provision of infrastructure services. The alleviation of these bottlenecks has also necessitated an increase in public capital expenditures, to an estimated average of 6 percent of GDP between 1990 and 1993.

In overall *financial performance*, the public enterprise sector in Thailand is profitable. Before-tax profits of the sector, as a share of GDP, have averaged between 2 and 3 percent, and the rate of return on the asset base has averaged about 5 percent. The main loss-making enterprises are in the transport sector (mass transit and railways), where prices are subject to controls.[30] However, these losses have been relatively small—they amounted to less than $1/10$ of 1 percent of GDP annually during the period under consideration. The most profitable public enterprises are the public utilities, which have significant monopoly power.

The basic conclusion is that, as with the other areas of structural reform discussed above, the "best practice" strategy may not have been followed, but initial distortions were relatively small and thus have not acted as a drag on long-term growth.

---

[30]The adjustment efforts of 1985–86 included several actions to raise public enterprises' prices (especially for oil and water supply) so as to improve profitability.

VIII   Conclusions

Thailand's adjustment experience during the past 15 years or so has, in general, been impressive. Despite having faced relatively large adverse external shocks in the late 1970s and early 1980s, Thailand, unlike many developing countries, did not experience a significant "investment pause" or a prolonged slowdown in growth following its stabilization program. It is clear, however, that the authorities were concerned at the time about a possible slowdown in growth in response to the adjustment policies. Belying even the most confident expectations, since 1986–87 Thailand has been in the midst of an unprecedented economic boom that has been characterized by rapid growth led by a surge in private investment and manufactured exports. This study has undertaken an examination of economic policies that may have contributed to this outcome.[31]

Common causes that underlie these developments include the following. First, there was a sustained improvement in external competitiveness. Because of the stabilization policy mix, particularly in the latter part of the adjustment period, expenditure and production switching was successful in generating rapid export-led growth. In particular, the nominal devaluation of 1984 was translated into a significant and sustained real depreciation, owing to the support of prudent financial management and a shift in the composition of public expenditures away from import-intensive capital spending. Second, the lack of labor market segmentation and the relatively high degree of labor mobility were instrumental in bringing about the resource movements necessary to generate the export boom. Moreover, the absence of wage-price inertia in goods and labor markets helped to keep Thailand's unit labor costs low relative to those of its trading partners, and this was an important factor (as suggested by the empirical analysis of investment behavior) in the relocation of production from other East Asian countries in the late 1980s. Third, the elimination of export taxes and the introduction of other incentives aimed at export promotion provided a highly favorable environment for private investors—both domestic and foreign. Fourth, the fiscal consolidation beginning in the mid-1980s, which resulted in substantial surpluses, made it possible to accommodate the surge in capital inflows and the investment boom in an environment of low inflation, and without a real appreciation of the baht. However, it appears that the scope for a major shift in the fiscal stance is becoming increasingly limited, making some upward pressure on the baht a possibility in the future.

Structural reforms, in general, did not conform closely to what are commonly regarded as "best practices." In particular, trade reforms did not follow a preannounced medium-term plan, and there were some policy reversals, including import tariff hikes for fiscal reasons. However, that the initial distortions were relatively small and that the authorities acted pragmatically in redressing problems before they became acute were important factors in preventing this from becoming a hindrance to long-term growth.

Although Thailand's adjustment experience does not necessarily provide a definitive blueprint for successful adjustment, and although not all of Thailand's policy choices proved to be unequivocally growth-enhancing, a few clear messages do emerge. First, Thailand began the period with relatively small macroeconomic imbalances and structural distortions, and therefore, despite suffering large adverse shocks, it faced a relatively less severe adjustment problem. Second, it had a well-developed and dynamic private sector and was thus able to generate a vigorous response to adjustment measures.

Finally, and most important, the authorities' high degree of policy credibility was attributable largely to the unwavering emphasis on macroeconomic stability, which was reinforced by a policy mix that was for the most part internally consistent. In turn, this meant that delays in effectively addressing the fiscal and external imbalances of the late 1970s and early 1980s, as well as the relatively slow progress of

---

[31]Although efforts to adjust to the external shocks and to correct the growing fiscal and external current account imbalances started in the early 1980s, at the beginning of what has been called the "adjustment" period throughout this paper, the major policy actions that can be most closely linked with the growth performance of the 1987–93 period did not take place until the mid-1980s.

structural reforms in certain key sectors, did not have a markedly detrimental effect on recovery and longer-term growth. It is undeniable that some of Thailand's economic performance is attributable to good fortune—"being at the right place at the right time"—particularly with respect to the substantial production relocation within Asia. It is equally true, however, that Thailand had the right policy environment in which to reap the benefits of these developments.

Appendix Private Investment Behavior in Thailand

This appendix presents results of an empirical investigation of the determinants of private investment in Thailand. During the 1970s and the first half of the 1980s, the ratio of private investment to GDP (in constant prices) remained more or less unchanged at about 20 percent. Since the second half of the 1980s, however, there has been a surge in private investment, which reached the equivalent of about 33 percent of GDP by 1993 (Figure 14). The discussion attempts to examine empirically the factors underlying the behavior of private investment in Thailand during the period 1970–93.

Specification Issues

General Considerations

Private investment in developing countries is typically specified as being a function of some or all of the following variables:[32] (1) changes in demand or economic activity, consistent with the accelerator model of capital accumulation; (2) relative prices of capital or labor (or both) to measure profitability; (3) the availability of financing to capture the effects of credit rationing and financial repression; (4) public sector investment to examine whether there is complementarity between public and private investment or whether public sector investment crowds out the private sector by preempting scarce physical and financial resources; (5) macroeconomic instability, proxied by the variability in inflation or real effective exchange rates; and (6) general measures of uncertainty, sometimes proxied by the debt-service ratio to measure the impact of the "debt overhang" on private investment behavior. In addition, in the case of Thailand, where a large part of the surge in private investment since the mid-1980s was due to the large inflows of foreign direct investment and where foreign borrowing has been an important source of financing for domestic investment, unit

labor costs in Thailand relative to its trading partners and foreign interest rates are included as explanatory variables.

The estimated equation thus takes the following general form:

$$LIP_t = \alpha_0 + \alpha_1 ACTY_t + \alpha_2 DINT_t + \alpha_3 CRED_t + \alpha_4 FINT_t + \alpha_5 LRULC_t + \alpha_6 LIPUB_t + \alpha_7 UNCERT_t + \alpha_8 LTOT_t + \alpha_9 FX_t + \alpha_{10} LIP_{t-1} + \epsilon_t, \quad (1)$$

where LIP is the logarithm of the ratio of private investment to GDP in constant prices;[33] $ACTY$ refers to the activity variable; $DINT$ stands for the domestic real interest rate to proxy for the cost of capital; and $CRED$ measures the availability of domestic financing; $FINT$ refers to the foreign real interest rates, adjusted for expected exchange rate changes; $LRULC$ stands for the logarithm of the index of unit labor costs in Thailand relative to its trading partners; and $LIPUB$ is the logarithm of the ratio of public sector investment to GDP in constant prices; FX stands for international reserves and serves as a proxy for the availability of foreign exchange; $UNCERT$ refers to the various possible proxies of macroeconomic instability or uncertainty, such as the variance in inflation rates and debt-service ratios; and $LTOT$ stands for the logarithm of the external terms of trade.

Testing for Stationarity

Before turning to the specific form of the investment function for Thailand, the key time-series properties of the variables to be included need to be examined. In particular, it is necessary to test whether the data are generated by stationary time-series processes.[34] Using nonstationary time series,

---

[32]Serven and Solimano (1994) have presented a detailed discussion of the theory and empirics of private investment behavior in developing countries.

[33]Using the level of private investment as the dependent variable could lead to spurious results with aggregate demand or the economic activity variable acting as a trend.

[34]A time series is said to be strictly stationary if all of its moments (mean, variance, and so forth) are independent of time. Typically, the weaker concept of stationarity is used, which only requires that the first two moments are invariant with respect to time and that the autocorrelations depend only on the length of the lag between observations and not on the points in time at which these observations are made.

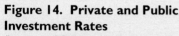

Figure 14. Private and Public Investment Rates

(In percent of GDP at constant prices)

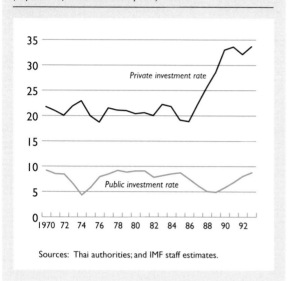

Sources: Thai authorities; and IMF staff estimates.

except under special circumstances, could lead to spurious results in the sense that regressing strongly trended variables on each other could overstate the "true" explanatory power of the regressors. Statistical tests for stationarity essentially involve testing whether $|\alpha| < 1$ in the equation $y_t = \alpha y_{t-1} + v_t$, or testing for a unit root in the process for y_t.

Indeed, the rationale for using the ratio of private investment to GDP as the dependent variable is to ensure stationarity. In the case of Thailand, however, as can be seen from Figure 14, there appears to have been a onetime "structural break" in the behavior of private investment around the mid-1980s. At first glance, there appears to be an indication that even the ratio is strongly trended, particularly in the later part of the sample period, suggesting the presence of a unit root.[35] The index of relative unit labor costs displays similar nonstationary behavior (see Figure 5 of the text) in the sample. All other variables considered as part of the general set of regressors were found to be stationary.

For the two variables for which casual observation suggests the presence of unit roots, "correlograms" were plotted (Figure 15) showing correlations between the series and its own lagged values. If a time series is stationary, the autocorrelations would be expected to decline quickly to values that are not significantly different from zero. Figure 15 shows that

both the investment ratio and relative unit labor costs are strongly autocorrelated, that the autocorrelations die out within five to seven lags, and that the pattern of autocorrelations is consistent with the data being generated by the autoregressive process of order 1 (or an AR(1) process).

Next, tests for unit roots of the type suggested by Perron (1989) were performed. Perron (1989) showed that standard tests may not reject the hypothesis of a unit root when the "true" data-generating mechanisms are that of stationary fluctuations around a trend that contains a onetime break. He derived a test that can distinguish between a process with a unit root and one that is a trend-stationary process but with a "permanent" break in the structure of the time series. These tests suggest that the hypothesis of unit roots for the two series in question can be rejected at the 1 percent significance level.[36]

Specification of Thailand's Investment Function

The choice of the activity or variable is influenced by the need to reduce the possibility of simultaneity biases that can arise because investment affects growth in the current period. In the case of Thailand, three economic activity variables were experimented with—lagged real GDP growth (*GRTH*), export volume growth (*EXGRTH*), and real GDP growth in partner countries (*FGRTH*).

INT was the domestic lending rate adjusted by actual inflation as measured by the consumer price index.

CRED was measured as the real growth of private sector credit. A priori, it is not clear whether a variable measuring the availability of financing should be included in the investment equation. On the one hand, although Thailand has had a financial system that is closer to the free market end of the developing country spectrum, government intervention remained an important feature of financial markets in Thailand until the early 1990s, when interest rates began to be deregulated. Although the lending ceilings may not have been binding for prime borrowers, there is evidence that smaller enterprises may have, at various times, had to queue for rationed credit. On the other hand, the scope for intervention has effectively been constrained by the relatively open capital account, especially for inflows. Thus,

---

[35]It should be noted, however, that by definition the ratio of private investment to GDP is inherently stationary in that it cannot grow without limit.

[36]The test statistics for the private investment ratio and the index of relative unit labor costs are estimated to be −5.77 and −8.32, respectively. The 1 percent critical value of the test statistic for the appropriate sample size, as calculated by Perron (1989), is −4.45, suggesting that the null hypothesis of the presence of a unit root can be rejected.

Figure 15. Private Investment Ratio and Relative Unit Labor Costs: Sample Autocorrelations

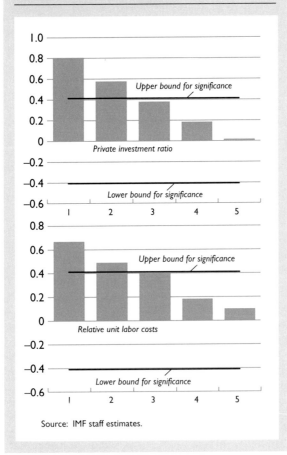

Source: IMF staff estimates.

interest rate ceilings could not be set so low as to persistently push domestic interest rates below the corresponding international rates. The inclusion of this variable in the investment function is, therefore, essentially an empirical issue and will be discussed further below.

The foreign interest rate (*FINT*) was measured as the U.S. prime lending rate adjusted by consumer price inflation in the United States and for the actual depreciation of the baht vis-à-vis the U.S. dollar.[37]

The relationship between private and public investment in Thailand was examined by including the ratio of public investment to GDP (*LIPUB*) and the

ratio of public infrastructure expenditure to GDP (*LIPUBI*) in the estimated equations.[38]

FX was measured as total international reserves (minus gold), expressed in months of imports.

The terms of trade (*LTOT*) were measured as the logarithm of the ratio of the price of exports to that of imports.

The two measures of instability or uncertainty that were used are *VINFL*, the variance of month-to-month consumer price inflation rates, and *LDSER*, the logarithm of the debt-service ratio.

A dummy variable was included to capture the impact of the shift in emphasis in the Board of Investment in the post-1986 period toward a proactive export- and private-sector-oriented strategy.

Results

Specification Search

The equation was estimated with annual data from 1970 to 1993 using ordinary least squares; the standard errors shown are heteroscedastic-consistent estimates.[39] The approach was to start by using the complete set of explanatory variables in the general equation (1) and to eliminate variables that were statistically insignificant. During this process, attention was also paid to the regression diagnostics, especially to the evidence on serial correlation and homoscedasticity of the residuals, since nonspherical errors in an equation that includes a lagged dependent variable give rise to inconsistent estimators.

The results of the different specifications of the equation are presented in Table 13. Key results of the specification search are the following. The coefficient on lagged real GDP growth, *GRTH*, was insignificant (Specification 1), as was that on the volume of export growth (not reported). The activity variable that was most accurately estimated and performed the best was *FGRTH*, the rate of real GDP growth in partner countries, and so it was used in subsequent specifications.[40] Thailand has always

---

[37]The expected rate of depreciation was proxied by the actual depreciation. In practice, since the baht was effectively pegged to the U.S. dollar throughout this period, this adjustment should not be expected to significantly affect the sign of the estimated coefficient.

[38]Public infrastructure investment was defined as capital expenditure by the central government and state enterprises on power, transport, and communication, and that by the central government on education, health, and agriculture.

[39]As is well known, estimation by ordinary least squares is less sensitive to specification errors in small samples than is estimation using instrumental-variables techniques. Further, instrumental-variables estimators are highly sensitive to the (often arbitrary) choice of instruments. This being said, care was taken to avoid potential simultaneity biases, particularly in the choice of the variable measuring economic activity, by using lagged real GDP growth or, in the case of Thailand, real GDP growth in trading-partner countries.

[40]These results do not imply that domestic activity levels, which are accounted for by expressing the dependent variable as an investment rate, are unimportant for private sector investment.

been a relatively open economy. This fact, coupled with the sharp acceleration in the growth in manufactured exports since 1986, is probably the reason for this finding.

As mentioned above, the inclusion of the *CRED* variable is primarily an empirical issue, since from a theoretical standpoint no clear-cut justification can be made in the case of Thailand for either including or excluding this variable. A key problem with including the volume of credit as an explanatory variable in an investment equation is that, if credit is in fact not constrained, then credit growth is determined by investment demand. In a statistical sense, there is the possibility that "causality" runs from the dependent variable to the independent variable, rendering the coefficient on the explanatory variable difficult to interpret.

The direction of causality was tested using "Granger-causality" tests. Granger (1969) introduced a concept of causality in which, broadly speaking, a variable y is said to be "Granger caused" by another variable x if current values of y can be predicted with better accuracy by using past values of x.[41] Testing for Granger causality essentially involves setting up a vector autoregression, in which all the variables of the system are expressed as linear functions of their own and each other's lagged values.[42] *F*-tests are then computed to test whether lagged values of any of the other variables enter a given equation significantly. Here, the vector autoregression was set up using the variables that enter the "preferred" specification.

Such tests reveal that, in the case of Thailand, the direction of causality seems to be from the growth of credit to investment rather than the other way around, implying that the coefficient on *CRED* in the estimated equation can be interpreted in the conventional way. However, the serially correlated and heteroscedastic residuals in Specifications 1 and 2 shown in Table 13 are evidence of equation misspecification. After some experimentation, it was found that residual serial correlation was no longer significant when the *CRED* variable was omitted from the regression. The exclusion of this variable had little significant impact on the coefficients on real growth in partner countries, relative unit labor costs, and real interest rates. However, the coefficient on the lagged dependent variable increased slightly while that on the public investment rate increased markedly, as did its statistical significance.

This latter result is indicative of collinearity between the *CRED* variable and *LIPUB* and is consistent with the finding (discussed below) of a negative coefficient on *LIPUB*.

Specification 3 shows that, besides the foreign growth variable, the two variables that are significant are *LRULC* and the ratio of public investment to GDP (*LIPUB*).[43] The coefficient on the relative unit labor cost variable implies that when Thailand's unit labor costs rise relative to its trading partners, private investment declines. The growing share of foreign-controlled investment in private investment and the increasing integration of the Thai economy into the world economy account for this relationship.

The negative coefficient on *LIPUB* suggests substitutability between public and private investment in Thailand, at least in the short term. This result may appear surprising, given that the provision of infrastructure has been a central theme of Thailand's development plans before the 1980s, and suggests that the coefficient needs to be interpreted carefully. In particular, it is useful to distinguish between investment spending and the stock of capital. The relatively well-developed stock of infrastructure was no doubt instrumental in supporting the boom in private investment in the late 1980s. It is also true, however, that during the second half of the 1970s and the early 1980s there was a rapid and somewhat uncoordinated expansion in public investment. Although much of this investment was concentrated in infrastructure-related sectors, any positive impact on private investment is likely to have materialized only with relatively long lags. In any event, such a relationship would not necessarily be captured by the contemporaneous correlation between public and private investment.

Figure 14 plots the public and private investment rates over the sample period. It shows that the negative relationship between public and private investment is, for the most part, explained by periods in which declines in public investment were accompanied by increases in private investment. This is particularly evident in the period since 1985, when the government began to significantly reduce and rationalize public investment spending; the resulting fiscal consolidation served to accommodate the acceleration in private investment in an environment of overall macroeconomic stability. The coefficients on these two variables were relatively robust to the addition and deletion of other variables in subsequent specifications.

---

[41]It is clear from this definition that this concept of causality does not necessarily imply an "event-outcome" relationship between the two variables.

[42]The variables that were included in the system are those that were statistically significant in the specification search outlined below.

[43]The results were very similar when public infrastructure investment was used. However, since the data on total public investment were judged to be more reliable, total public investment was used in the specification search.

Table 13. Private Investment Equations, 1970–93

Explanatory Variables	Specification Number 1	2	3	4	5	6	7	8
CONSTANT	0.718 (1.38)	0.438 (1.09)	0.533 (1.42)	0.501 (1.15)	0.345 (0.81)	0.393 (0.99)	0.031 (0.18)	0.001 (0.08)
GRTH(−1)	0.006 (0.10)							
FGRTH		0.021*** (3.00)	0.027*** (3.69)	0.028*** (5.03)	0.025*** (4.63)	0.025*** (4.89)	0.025*** (4.39)	0.026*** (5.12)
CRED	0.008*** (4.24)	0.006*** (3.09)						
RDINT	−0.009** (−2.01)	−0.007* (−1.97)	−0.002 (−0.31)	−0.003 (−0.34)	−0.003 (−0.97)	−0.003 (−1.14)	−0.005* (−1.93)	−0.005** (2.93)
LRULC	−0.234* (−1.98)	−0.194** (−2.24)	−0.248*** (−3.47)	−0.246*** (−3.14)	−0.251*** (−3.60)	−0.254*** (−4.54)	−0.208*** (−5.89)	−0.220*** (−7.11)
LIPUB	0.070 (0.81)	−0.009 (−0.11)	−0.173** (−2.50)	−0.175** (−2.54)	−0.144** (−2.74)	−0.143*** (−2.76)	−0.167*** (−3.69)	−0.182*** (−5.00)
VINFL	−0.002 (−1.17)	— (0.01)						
LFX	0.016 (0.33)	−0.137 (−0.81)	−0.065 (−1.15)	−0.063 (−1.15)				
LTOT	−0.066 (−0.29)		0.050 (0.31)	0.046 (0.28)	−0.032 (−0.24)			
LDSER	−0.089 (−1.37)	−0.070 (−1.19)	−0.095 (−1.45)	−0.091 (−1.15)	−0.076 (−0.89)	−0.075 (−0.91)		
RFINT	— (−0.09)	— (−0.23)	— (−0.33)	— (−0.23)	— (−0.14)	— (−0.32)	— (−0.34)	
LIP(−1)	0.468** (2.93)	0.602*** (5.24)	0.702*** (4.19)	0.704*** (4.05)	0.605*** (4.57)	0.598*** (4.49)	0.708*** (8.71)	0.676*** (8.92)
Adjusted R^2	0.89	0.92	0.89	0.90	0.90	0.89	0.91	0.94
Durbin's H for serial correlation	0.54	−0.71	−0.36	−0.37	0.03	0.01	0.13	0.02
(p-value)[1]	0.59	0.11	0.72	0.71	0.98	0.99	0.89	0.99
Augmented Dickey-Fuller test statistic	−5.39	−5.17	−4.77	−4.73	−4.29	−4.29	−4.16	−4.31
(p-value)[2]	—	—	—	—	—	—	—	0.01
F-statistic (zero slopes)	16.22	23.09	17.88	21.65	24.49	30.05	35.04	50.41
(p-value)[3]	—	—	—	—	—	—	—	—
Jarque-Bera normality test statistic	0.97	1.64	0.27	0.17	0.35	0.34	1.00	0.26
(p-value)[4]	0.62	0.44	0.88	0.92	0.84	0.84	0.59	0.88
Breusch-Pagan heteroscedasticity test statistic	10.29	13.51	11.08	8.40	5.34	5.57	3.97	2.09
(p-value)[5]	0.50	0.26	0.35	0.49	0.72	0.59	0.68	0.92

Source: IMF staff estimates.

Note: The dependent variable was the logarithm of the ratio of private investment to GDP in constant prices (LIP); LIP(−1) is LIP lagged by one period; t-statistics are shown in parentheses; * indicates significance at the 10 percent level, ** indicates significance at the 5 percent level, and *** indicates significance at the 1 percent level. GRTH is real GDP growth in Thailand; FGRTH is real GDP growth in Thailand's trading partners; CRED is the growth of real private sector credit; RDINT is the domestic real lending rate; RFINT is the real U.S. prime lending rate; LRULC is the logarithm of relative unit labor costs; LIPUB is the ratio of public investment to GDP; VINFL is the variance in the month-to-month inflation rate of the consumer price index; LDSER is the logarithm of the external debt-service ratio; LFX is the logarithm of the import coverage of foreign exchange reserves; and DTOT is percentage change in the terms of trade.

[1] The probability of accepting the null hypothesis that the residuals are not serially correlated.
[2] The probability of accepting the null hypothesis that the residuals have a unit root.
[3] The probability of accepting the null hypothesis that all slopes are equal to zero.
[4] The probability of accepting the null hypothesis that the residuals are normally distributed.
[5] The probability of accepting the null hypothesis that the residuals are homoscedastic.

The real interest rate (*RDINT*) entered the equation with a negative sign but was less robust than *LRULC* and *LIPUB* across specifications. Indeed, the decline in private investment in the mid-1980s is attributable to the sharp increase in interest rates when a conservative monetary policy stance was adopted (see Section V of the text).

The measure of instability (*VINFL*) was statistically insignificant (Specification 3). This is attributable to the fact that Thailand has had low and stable inflation for virtually all of the sample, with only very short-lived accelerations following the two oil shocks. The availability of foreign exchange (*FX*) (Specifications 3 and 4) was also statistically insignificant. Despite the secular decline that Thailand experienced in its external terms of trade during the period under study, the coefficient on *LTOT* was found to be statistically insignificant (Specifications 3, 4, and 5). The debt-service ratio was similarly found to be statistically insignificant (Specifications 3, 4, 5, and 6). Finally, the foreign interest rate variable, which was consistently insignificant, was omitted.[44]

Specification 8 in Table 13 was chosen as the preferred equation. All the variables in that specification have the expected sign and are statistically significant. The diagnostics on the regression suggest that the hypotheses of serially uncorrelated and homoscedastic errors cannot be rejected. The coefficient on the activity variable suggests that a 1 percentage point increase in trading partners' real GDP growth would result in an increase in the ratio of private investment to GDP of 0.7 percent. The coefficient on real domestic interest rates suggests that a 1 percentage point increase in real interest rates would lower the ratio of private investment to GDP by about 0.1 percent, while an increase in public investment by the equivalent of 1 percentage point of GDP would decrease the private investment rate by 0.5 percent. The coefficient on relative unit labor costs suggests that a 1 percentage point decrease in Thailand's relative unit labor costs would result in an almost equivalent increase in the ratio of the private investment rate to GDP. Figure 16 shows that the ratio of private investment implied by the estimated equation tracks the actual ratio quite closely and accurately predicts the important turning point in 1986.

---

[44]The dummy variable for the post-1986 period was always insignificant, possibly because any influence of the shift toward active export promotion, through the devaluation and the elimination of export taxes, is being captured in the relative unit labor cost variable. The relative price of capital goods (proxied by the ratio of the fixed investment deflator to the GDP deflator) was also used instead of the domestic real interest rate but proved to be insignificant in all specifications.

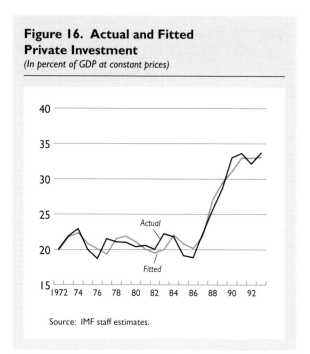

Figure 16. Actual and Fitted Private Investment
(In percent of GDP at constant prices)

Source: IMF staff estimates.

Recursive Estimation

Once the "preferred" specification was arrived at, a recursive estimation procedure was implemented to test the robustness of the parameter estimates over time. In view of the possibility that the structure of the economy has undergone significant changes over the past two and a half decades, the assumption of time-invariant parameters may not be supported by the data. Figure 17 shows the behavior of the estimated coefficients when the sample begins in 1972 and ends in the year shown on the horizontal axis (forward recursive estimates). The charts show that the estimated coefficients are relatively stable over time. The exception is the coefficient on the lagged dependent variable, which goes from being close to zero in the first part of the sample to being significantly different from zero in the later part of the sample, implying that the degree of autocorrelation in the private investment ratio has increased over time. This finding is not inconsistent with the apparent "regime" change characterized by the increase in the private investment rate to a permanently higher level, and with the fact that the later part of the sample covers the period of transition from one "regime" to the other.

Relative Contributions of Explanatory Variables

Table 14 shows the contributions of the explanatory variables to the estimated change in private in-

Table 14. Contribution of Explanatory Variables to Estimated Changes in Private Investment

Explanatory Variables	Estimated Coefficient	Estimated Change in I/GDP due to:[1]	1987–93 Share of Estimated Change due to:[2]	Long-run Elasticities with respect to:
Constant	0.001			
Real GDP growth in trading partners	0.026	–1.3	–12.0	0.08
Real domestic interest rates	–0.005	0.7	6.5	–0.02
Relative unit labor costs	–0.220	3.0	26.8	–0.68
Ratio of public investment to GDP (in constant prices)	–0.182	–1.0	–8.5	–0.56
Lagged dependent variable	0.676	9.8	87.1	
Total		11.2	100.0	
Actual change in dependent variable		11.4		
Share of actual change explained by regression		98.5		
Share of actual change explained by residual		1.5		

Source: IMF staff estimates.
Note: The dependent variable was the ratio of private investment to GDP in constant prices (I/GDP).
[1]In percentage points of GDP.
[2]In percent.

vestment during the postadjustment period (1987–93).[45] The decline in real GDP growth in partner countries and the increase in public investment in the early 1990s were negative influences on private investment in the postadjustment phase, while the fall in real lending rates throughout this period had a positive impact on private investment. The decline in relative unit labor costs made a significant positive contribution, accounting for about a fourth of the acceleration in private investment. The large share of the lagged dependent variable suggests an increase in "inertia" in the evolution of private investment—a development that appears, prima facie, to be inconsistent with an increasingly dynamic economy. A possible explanation could be that there was a change in the composition of invest-

ment—toward high-technology industries—as a result of the production relocation that took place from other East Asian countries, and that the technology gap resulted in higher costs, at least initially, of adjusting the capital stock.

Simulations

The movement in relative unit labor costs in Thailand appears to be an important variable in explaining the evolution of private investment, especially in the post-1986 period. The decline in relative unit labor costs in Thailand (Figure 18) during this period was driven by the currency realignments in the area and by rising labor costs in other countries. With the yen appreciation between 1985 and 1988, production was increasingly shifted to Thailand (and to Malaysia and the other NIEs). Subsequent appreciations of the currencies of some of the NIEs, rising wage costs in Japan, Korea, and Taiwan Province of China, and the depreciation of the baht along with the U.S. dollar were also instrumental in shifting production to Thailand. To examine the importance of this variable in explaining the behavior of private investment since the second half of the 1980s, a simulation exercise was performed in which relative

---

[45]The last IMF stand-by arrangement, scheduled to expire in March 1987, was canceled at the end of 1986. The decomposition was also calculated for the period 1972–87 and for the "preadjustment" (pre-1980) and "adjustment" (1980–86) periods separately. However, in view of the very small degree of variation in the private investment ratio and in most of the explanatory variables (with the exception of relative unit labor costs) before 1986–87, this exercise did not result in a meaningful decomposition and is not reported here.

Figure 17. Recursive Estimates (Forward Recursions)
(Sample starts in year shown on x-axis and ends in 1993)

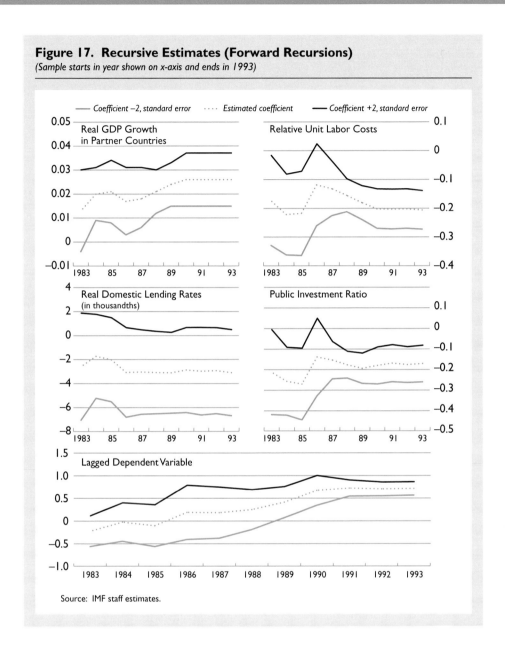

Source: IMF staff estimates.

unit labor costs were assumed to be unchanged at the average level in 1984–85.[46] Figure 19 shows the actual and simulated behavior of private investment. Clearly, the evolution of relative labor costs in Thailand has been a very important factor in private investment behavior, particularly since 1989. Had labor costs in Thailand relative to its trading partners remained at their level in 1984–85, private invest-

ment would, other things being equal, have been lower by the equivalent of over 4 percentage points of GDP.

Concluding Remarks

The key messages that emerge from this analysis are the following. First, while some of the surge in private investment in the second half of the 1980s could be ascribed to fortuitous exogenous developments, policy actions taken by the Thai authorities—including the devaluation of the baht and the elimination of export taxes and granting of export

---

[46]This is a "ceteris paribus" simulation, in which all other coefficients and variables are assumed to remain invariant in this counterfactual scenario. This is clearly a strong assumption, but the results are nevertheless useful in gauging the importance of the evolution of particular variables in the estimated equation.

Figure 18. Unit Labor Costs in Thailand and Selected Countries
(Indices, 1985 = 100)

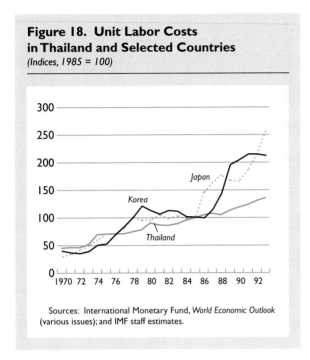

Sources: International Monetary Fund, *World Economic Outlook* (various issues); and IMF staff estimates.

Figure 19. Actual and Simulated Private Investment
(In percent of GDP at constant prices)

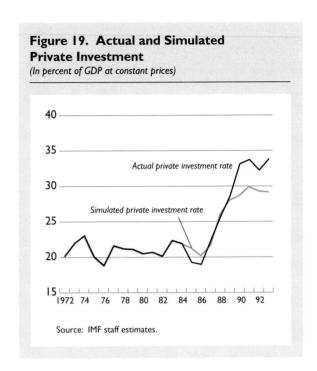

Source: IMF staff estimates.

incentives—contributed significantly. Second, the decline in interest rates following the period of relatively tight monetary conditions in the immediate aftermath of the devaluation was also important. Prudent financial management and a largely internally consistent policy mix were also instrumental in translating the nominal devaluation into a sustained real depreciation and in enhancing policy credibility. Third, flexible labor markets (in terms of real wage flexibility and labor mobility) were important factors underlying the developments in relative unit labor costs and, in turn, the increase in investment. Fourth, the surge in private investment could be accommodated without a significant acceleration in inflation through most of the period because of the simultaneous fiscal consolidation, in which public expenditures (especially on investment) were rationalized.

Finally, although not all of these effects are explicitly accounted for in the estimated investment equation because of the lack of measurable proxies, a hallmark of macroeconomic developments in Thailand has been the high priority accorded to overall macroeconomic stability. This, combined with the pro-business orientation of economic policymakers (despite several changes in government), resulted in relatively low policy uncertainty and has proven to be conducive to private investment, both domestic and foreign.[47]

---

[47]The finding that the various measures of uncertainty that were included were always insignificant is consistent with this conclusion.

References

Anand, Ritu, and Sweder van Wijnbergen, 1989, "Inflation and the Financing of Government Expenditure: An Introductory Analysis with an Application to Turkey," *World Bank Economic Review,* Vol. 3 (January), pp. 17–38.

Barro, Robert J., 1989, "Economic Growth in a Cross Section of Countries," NBER Working Paper 3120 (Cambridge, Mass.: National Bureau of Economic Research, September).

Barro, Robert J., and Jong-Wha Lee, 1993, "International Comparisons of Educational Attainment," *Journal of Monetary Economics,* Vol. 32 (December), pp. 363–94.

Bercuson, Kenneth, and Linda M. Koenig, 1993, "The Recent Surge in Capital Inflows to Three Asian Countries: Causes and Macroeconomic Impact," Occasional Paper 15 (Kuala Lumpur: South-East Asian Central Banks, Research and Training Centre).

Bertrand, Trent, and Lyn Squire, 1980, "The Relevance of the Dual Economy Model: A Case Study of Thailand," *Oxford Economic Papers,* Vol. 32 (November), pp. 480–511.

Bhattacharya, Amarendra, and Johannes F. Linn, 1988, "Trade and Industrial Policies in the Developing Countries of East Asia," World Bank Discussion Paper 27 (Washington: World Bank).

Bruno, Michael, 1985, "Aggregate Supply and Demand Factors in OECD Unemployment: An Update," NBER Working Paper 1696 (Cambridge, Mass.: National Bureau of Economic Research).

Bruno, Michael, and William Easterly, 1995, "Inflation Crises and Long-Run Growth," NBER Working Paper 5209 (Cambridge, Mass.: National Bureau of Economic Research).

Bruno, Michael, and Jeffrey Sachs, 1985, *The Economics of Worldwide Stagflation* (Cambridge, Mass.: Harvard University Press).

Dean, Judith M., Seema Desai, and James Riedel, 1994, "Trade Policy Reform in Developing Countries since 1985," World Bank Discussion Paper 267 (Washington: World Bank).

Elias, Victor, 1991, "The Role of Total Factor Productivity on Economic Growth," background paper for the *World Development Report* (unpublished; Washington: World Bank).

Fischer, Stanley, 1993, "The Role of Macroeconomic Factors in Growth," *Journal of Monetary Economics,* Vol. 32 (December), pp. 485–512.

Goldsbrough, David, Sharmini Coorey, Louis Dicks-Mireaux, Balazs Horvath, Kalpana Kochhar, Mauro Mecagni, Erik Offerdal, and Jianping Zhou, 1996, *Reinvigorating Growth in Developing Countries: Lessons from Adjustment Policies in Eight Economies,* Occasional Paper 139 (Washington: International Monetary Fund, July).

Granger, C.W.J., 1969, "Investigating Causal Relations by Econometric Models and Cross-Spectral Methods," *Econometrica,* Vol. 37 (July), pp. 424–38.

Heller, Peter S., Richard D. Haas, and Ahsan S. Mansur, 1986, *A Review of the Fiscal Impulse Measure,* Occasional Paper 44 (Washington: International Monetary Fund, May).

International Monetary Fund, various years, *Government Finance Statistics Yearbook* (Washington).

———, various years, *International Financial Statistics* (Washington).

———, various years, *World Economic Outlook* (Washington).

King, Robert G., and Ross Levine, 1994, "Capital Fundamentalism, Economic Development and Economic Growth," *Carnegie-Rochester Series on Public Policy,* Vol. 40 (June), pp. 259–300.

Knight, Malcolm, Norman Loayza, and Delano Villanueva, 1992, "Testing the Neoclassical Theory of Economic Growth: A Panel Data Approach," IMF Working Paper 92/106 (Washington: International Monetary Fund).

Mankiw, N. Gregory, David Romer, and David N. Weil, 1992, "A Contribution to the Empirics of Economic Growth," *Quarterly Journal of Economics,* Vol. 107 (May), pp. 407–38.

McCarthy, F. Desmond, J. Peter Neary, and Giovanni Zanalda, 1994, "Measuring the Effect of External Shocks and the Policy Response to Them: Empirical Methodology Applied to the Philippines," Policy Research Working Paper 1271 (Washington: World Bank, March).

Nehru, Vikram, and Ashok Dhareshwar, 1993, "A New Database on Physical Capital Stock: Sources, Methodology, and Results," *Revista de Análisis Económico,* Vol. 8 (No. 1), pp. 37–59.

Perron, Philippe, 1989, "The Great Crash, the Oil Price Shock, and the Unit Root Hypothesis," *Econometrica,* Vol. 57 (November), pp. 1361–1401.

Robinson, David, Yangho Byeon, and Ranjit Teja, with Wanda Tseng, 1991, *Thailand: Adjusting to Success—Current Policy Issues,* Occasional Paper 85 (Washington: International Monetary Fund, August).

Sarel, Michael, 1995,"Demographic Dynamics and the Empirics of Economic Growth," *Staff Papers,* International Monetary Fund, Vol. 42 (June) pp. 398–410.

Schadler, Susan, Maria Carkovic, Adam Bennett, and Robert Kahn, 1993, *Recent Experiences with Surges in Capital Inflows,* Occasional Paper 108 (Washington: International Monetary Fund, December).

Serven, Luis, and Andrés Solimano, 1994, *Striving for Growth After Adjustment: The Role of Capital Formation* (Washington: World Bank).

Summers, Robert, and Alan Heston, 1991, "The Penn World Table (Mark 5): An Expanded Set of International Comparisons, 1950–88," *Quarterly Journal of Economics,* Vol. 106 (May), No. 2, pp. 327–68. An updated version of the Penn World Tables, Mark 5.6 (available from NBER Publications, 1050 Massachusetts Avenue, Cambridge, Mass. 02138) was used for the regressions in this Occasional Paper.

Tinakorn, Pranee, and C. Sussangkarn, 1994, "Productivity Growth in Thailand" (unpublished; Bangkok: Thailand Development Research Institute).

World Bank, 1991, *World Development Report* (New York: Oxford University Press).

_____, various years, *World Tables* (Baltimore, Md.: Johns Hopkins University Press).

_____, various years, *World Debt Tables* (Washington).

Recent Occasional Papers of the International Monetary Fund

146. Thailand: The Road to Sustained Growth, by Kalpana Kochhar, Louis Dicks-Mireaux, Balazs Horvath, Mauro Mecagni, Erik Offerdal, and Jianping Zhou. 1996.

145. Exchange Rate Movements and Their Impact on Trade and Investment in the APEC Region, by Takatoshi Ito, Peter Isard, Steven Symansky, and Tamim Bayoumi. 1996.

144. National Bank of Poland: The Road to Indirect Instruments, by Piero Ugolini. 1996.

143. Adjustment for Growth: The African Experience, by Michael T. Hadjimichael, Michael Nowak, Robert Sharer, and Amor Tahari. 1996.

142. Quasi-Fiscal Operations of Public Financial Institutions, by G.A. Mackenzie and Peter Stella. 1996.

141. Monetary and Exchange System Reforms in China: An Experiment in Gradualism, by Hassanali Mehran, Marc Quintyn, Tom Nordman, and Bernard Laurens. 1996.

140. Government Reform in New Zealand, by Graham C. Scott. 1996.

139. Reinvigorating Growth in Developing Countries: Lessons from Adjustment Policies in Eight Economies, by David Goldsbrough, Sharmini Coorey, Louis Dicks-Mireaux, Balazs Horvath, Kalpana Kochhar, Mauro Mecagni, Erik Offerdal, and Jianping Zhou. 1996.

138. Aftermath of the CFA Franc Devaluation, by Jean A.P. Clément, with Johannes Mueller, Stéphane Cossé, and Jean Le Dem. 1996.

137. The Lao People's Democratic Republic: Systemic Transformation and Adjustment, edited by Ichiro Otani and Chi Do Pham. 1996.

136. Jordan: Strategy for Adjustment and Growth, edited by Edouard Maciejewski and Ahsan Mansur. 1996.

135. Vietnam: Transition to a Market Economy, by John R. Dodsworth, Erich Spitäller, Michael Braulke, Keon Hyok Lee, Kenneth Miranda, Christian Mulder, Hisanobu Shishido, and Krishna Srinivasan. 1996.

134. India: Economic Reform and Growth, by Ajai Chopra, Charles Collyns, Richard Hemming, and Karen Parker with Woosik Chu and Oliver Fratzscher. 1995.

133. Policy Experiences and Issues in the Baltics, Russia, and Other Countries of the Former Soviet Union, edited by Daniel A. Citrin and Ashok K. Lahiri. 1995.

132. Financial Fragilities in Latin America: The 1980s and 1990s, by Liliana Rojas-Suárez and Steven R. Weisbrod. 1995.

131. Capital Account Convertibility: Review of Experience and Implications for IMF Policies, by staff teams headed by Peter J. Quirk and Owen Evans. 1995.

130. Challenges to the Swedish Welfare State, by Desmond Lachman, Adam Bennett, John H. Green, Robert Hagemann, and Ramana Ramaswamy. 1995.

129. IMF Conditionality: Experience Under Stand-By and Extended Arrangements. Part II: Background Papers. Susan Schadler, Editor, with Adam Bennett, Maria Carkovic, Louis Dicks-Mireaux, Mauro Mecagni, James H.J. Morsink, and Miguel A. Savastano. 1995.

128. IMF Conditionality: Experience Under Stand-By and Extended Arrangements. Part I: Key Issues and Findings, by Susan Schadler, Adam Bennett, Maria Carkovic, Louis Dicks-Mireaux, Mauro Mecagni, James H.J. Morsink, and Miguel A. Savastano. 1995.

127. Road Maps of the Transition: The Baltics, the Czech Republic, Hungary, and Russia, by Biswajit Banerjee, Vincent Koen, Thomas Krueger, Mark S. Lutz, Michael Marrese, and Tapio O. Saavalainen. 1995.

126. The Adoption of Indirect Instruments of Monetary Policy, by a staff team headed by William E. Alexander, Tomás J.T. Baliño, and Charles Enoch. 1995.

125. United Germany: The First Five Years—Performance and Policy Issues, by Robert Corker, Robert A. Feldman, Karl Habermeier, Hari Vittas, and Tessa van der Willigen. 1995.

124. Saving Behavior and the Asset Price "Bubble" in Japan: Analytical Studies, edited by Ulrich Baumgartner and Guy Meredith. 1995.

123. Comprehensive Tax Reform: The Colombian Experience, edited by Parthasarathi Shome. 1995.

122. Capital Flows in the APEC Region, edited by Mohsin S. Khan and Carmen M. Reinhart. 1995.

121. Uganda: Adjustment with Growth, 1987–94, by Robert L. Sharer, Hema R. De Zoysa, and Calvin A. McDonald. 1995.

120. Economic Dislocation and Recovery in Lebanon, by Sena Eken, Paul Cashin, S. Nuri Erbas, Jose Martelino, and Adnan Mazarei. 1995.

119. Singapore: A Case Study in Rapid Development, edited by Kenneth Bercuson with a staff team comprising Robert G. Carling, Aasim M. Husain, Thomas Rumbaugh, and Rachel van Elkan. 1995.

118. Sub-Saharan Africa: Growth, Savings, and Investment, by Michael T. Hadjimichael, Dhaneshwar Ghura, Martin Mühleisen, Roger Nord, and E. Murat Uçer. 1995.

117. Resilience and Growth Through Sustained Adjustment: The Moroccan Experience, by Saleh M. Nsouli, Sena Eken, Klaus Enders, Van-Can Thai, Jörg Decressin, and Filippo Cartiglia, with Janet Bungay. 1995.

116. Improving the International Monetary System: Constraints and Possibilities, by Michael Mussa, Morris Goldstein, Peter B. Clark, Donald J. Mathieson, and Tamim Bayoumi. 1994.

115. Exchange Rates and Economic Fundamentals: A Framework for Analysis, by Peter B. Clark, Leonardo Bartolini, Tamim Bayoumi, and Steven Symansky. 1994.

114. Economic Reform in China: A New Phase, by Wanda Tseng, Hoe Ee Khor, Kalpana Kochhar, Dubravko Mihaljek, and David Burton. 1994.

113. Poland: The Path to a Market Economy, by Liam P. Ebrill, Ajai Chopra, Charalambos Christofides, Paul Mylonas, Inci Otker, and Gerd Schwartz. 1994.

112. The Behavior of Non-Oil Commodity Prices, by Eduardo Borensztein, Mohsin S. Khan, Carmen M. Reinhart, and Peter Wickham. 1994.

111. The Russian Federation in Transition: External Developments, by Benedicte Vibe Christensen. 1994.

110. Limiting Central Bank Credit to the Government: Theory and Practice, by Carlo Cottarelli. 1993.

109. The Path to Convertibility and Growth: The Tunisian Experience, by Saleh M. Nsouli, Sena Eken, Paul Duran, Gerwin Bell, and Zühtü Yücelik. 1993.

108. Recent Experiences with Surges in Capital Inflows, by Susan Schadler, Maria Carkovic, Adam Bennett, and Robert Kahn. 1993.

107. China at the Threshold of a Market Economy, by Michael W. Bell, Hoe Ee Khor, and Kalpana Kochhar with Jun Ma, Simon N'guiamba, and Rajiv Lall. 1993.

106. Economic Adjustment in Low-Income Countries: Experience Under the Enhanced Structural Adjustment Facility, by Susan Schadler, Franek Rozwadowski, Siddharth Tiwari, and David O. Robinson. 1993.

105. The Structure and Operation of the World Gold Market, by Gary O'Callaghan. 1993.

104. Price Liberalization in Russia: Behavior of Prices, Household Incomes, and Consumption During the First Year, by Vincent Koen and Steven Phillips. 1993.

103. Liberalization of the Capital Account: Experiences and Issues, by Donald J. Mathieson and Liliana Rojas-Suárez. 1993.

102. Financial Sector Reforms and Exchange Arrangements in Eastern Europe. Part I: Financial Markets and Intermediation, by Guillermo A. Calvo and Manmohan S. Kumar. Part II: Exchange Arrangements of Previously Centrally Planned Economies, by Eduardo Borensztein and Paul R. Masson. 1993.

101. Spain: Converging with the European Community, by Michel Galy, Gonzalo Pastor, and Thierry Pujol. 1993.

Note: For information on the title and availability of Occasional Papers not listed, please consult the IMF Publications Catalog or contact IMF Publication Services.